How to Find the Best Eldercare

How to Find the Best Eldercare

Marilyn Rantz, PhD, RN, FAAN

and

Mary Zwygart-Stauffacher, PhD, RN, FAAN

Fairview Press
Minneapolis

Published by Fairview Press, 2450 Riverside Avenue,
Minneapolis, Minnesota 55454.

Library of Congress Cataloging-in-Publication Data
Rantz, Marilyn J.
How to find the best eldercare / Marilyn Rantz and Mary Zwygart-Stauffacher.
p. cm. — (How to find the best nursing home)
ISBN-13: 978-1-57749-190-3 (alk. paper)
ISBN-10: 1-57749-190-4 (alk. paper)
1. Older people—Care—United States. 2. Older people—Long-term care—United States. 3. Long-term care facilities—United States. I. Zwygart-Stauffacher, Mary, 1955- II. Title.
HV1461.R36 2009
362.610973—dc22

2009003908

First Printing: 2009
Printed in the United States of America
13 12 11 10 09 7 6 5 4 3 2 1

Cover design: Laurie Ingram
Interior design: Ryan Scheife, Mayfly Design (www.mayflydesign.net)

For a free current catalog of Fairview Press titles, please call toll free 1-800-544-8207. Or visit our Web site at www.fairviewpress.org.

CONTENTS

CHAPTER FOUR

Assisted Living: Making a Decision about Quality of Care and Services *41*

These facilities can be a good choice for elders who need some help with personal care, such as bathing, meals, laundry, medications, and housekeeping. The better facilities are homelike, have a caring staff, and provide plenty of choices when it comes to food and activities.

CHAPTER FIVE

Nursing Homes: Making a Decision about Quality of Care *103*

The most progressive nursing homes have moved away from an institutional look and feel to offer personalized care in attractive facilities that also welcome families into their routines.

FOREWORD

Choosing long-term care services is like other big changes and choices you have managed throughout your life: leaving home, finding a place to live, choosing education and professional training, bringing up children, working. In fact, you have the ability to make this next choice for yourself or your parent or friend. *How to Find the Best Eldercare* makes the decisions easier by laying out the options you will have, whether for in-home care, senior housing, assisted living, or nursing home care. In fact, as your needs change, you may move from one arrangement to another—from in-home help to senior housing to a nursing home and so on. What's most important for you is finding the best of each of these services. One way to do that is to be able to cross off, as quickly as possible, options that simply will not meet your care and comfort needs, while identifying those services or institutions you might examine more closely.

The decision to look for long-term care services—whether it be allowing people to come into your home to help with cleaning and care or moving into assisted living or a nursing home—can be heart-wrenching. With many headlines exposing the problems people have in getting appropriate and compassionate care, some people tell their families never to let them get to the point that such decisions need to be made. And family members typically agree, reassuring the person that they will be there for them, so they won't need to worry about that. As a result, there is often little or no planning for what to do if a crisis occurs and a nursing home or assisted-living residence becomes the best option for the complexity of care or assistance that is needed. Furthermore, there are few good guidelines that individuals and families can use to assist them with determining and planning for the quality of services that can be anticipated.

In-home services may be a good option for some. For instance, if daily living chores become overwhelming, the local Meals on Wheels program makes sure the person gets daily nutrition, and a home health aide can provide help with bathing, preparing meals, and cleaning. In most communities there are also other services that can be helpful, such as those provided by social workers and those who do home maintenance. In some locations registered nurses can be employed as care managers to help the older person maintain health and independent living. Sometimes, however, the available services are just not enough to provide the healthcare and assistance needed for someone to remain at home. In those instances, an assisted-living facility or nursing home can be a good option. There are assisted-living residences and nursing homes in the United States that provide good and even great care. The challenge is in knowing how to find them. With *How to Find the Best Eldercare*, you can quickly locate the better assisted-living or nursing homes in your area by taking a simple, twenty- to thirty-minute walk-through at different facilities. Even if your choice must be hurried, there are a number of things you can do to select a facility that meets the needs of the older person and the family.

How to Find the Best Eldercare is based on the "Walk-Through Observation Guides" developed by Marilyn Rantz, Mary Zwygart-Stauffacher, and other colleagues to help assisted-living residences and nursing homes evaluate and improve their quality of care. When families began asking them for help in finding a facility, they knew it was time to bring this resource to consumers. The response has been tremendous: "This guide really works! I don't know what I would have done without it. With some nursing homes, I just walked in, turned around, and walked out again, but I kept on looking. We found a wonderful place. Mom is getting the care she needs, the staff is good, and the food and activities are good. We know no place is perfect, but we think we have found a good one. Thanks for your help!"

This book will help you sort the good nursing homes from the poor ones, focusing on the positive and approaching the assisted-living or nursing home experience without fear. If your needs are not met, this book can help you contact the long-term care ombudsman services and citizen advocacy groups in your state. You will know how to check the Web sites of consumer advocacy organizations, to be sure that the facility you are considering is not currently in financial trouble or accused of providing substandard care. This book shows you how to locate available state and federal government information to assure that the facility you are considering is doing a good job. No matter how good care is in a facility, a change in administrator or owner can alter a facility dramatically. There is no good way to protect against this, but if a facility is constantly changing ownership, it is not a good sign.

How to Find the Best Eldercare will also help you identify good assisted-living facilities, as well as other options such as in-home services, hospice, and senior housing. This resource is unique not only because it helps you negotiate the maze of long-term care services that are available in most communities today but also because it helps you make judgments about the quality of those services. It is not enough to find a service or facility. You also need to be sure it is a good one in which services are provided by experienced, qualified, and caring staff who enjoy their work, are satisfied with their job, and have reasonable longevity with their employer.

Making the right choice for long-term care is a difficult and often discouraging and disheartening task for an older person and the person's family and friends. Making the choice, though, is not unlike other choices you and your family or friends have made in life. This consumer guide makes choosing long-term care much easier. It has the potential to help millions of older persons and their surrogates make informed choices so that older persons receive the quality of care and life that they deserve. The better informed the public is, the less likely it is that poor or inadequate care will be tolerated, and the more likely it is that the long-term care sector will continue to improve the quality of care and life it provides for older citizens.

—Sarah Greene Burger, RN,C, MPH, FAAN
Coordinator of the Coalition of Geriatric Nursing Organizations
Hartford Institute for Geriatric Nursing Organizations

—Meridean L. Maas, PhD, RN, FAAN
Professor Emerita
Co-Director, The John A. Hartford Center of Geriatric Nursing Excellence
College of Nursing
The University of Iowa

PREFACE

Although family and friends provide most long-term care, this book will help when your care needs exceed what you and your family and friends can do for you, or what you can do for your loved one. Long-term care options are changing. Consumers are demanding better services, more amenities, and, above all, more caring and competent staff. In many communities across the country, options are emerging to help older adults and those with chronic care needs. These include senior housing, residential care, assisted living, adult daycare, in-home care, and companion services. These competing services are driving long-term care facilities to change for the better—to become more personalized and homelike.

But consumers often are perplexed by the maze of options and the difficulties of finding the right option for themselves or a loved one. This book will help consumers not only identify the various care services available but also—and more important—find the highest quality of care available. Lots of services can provide some help and some care, but what you or your loved one deserves is *high-quality care.* This book will help you get that.

The one-of-a-kind questionnaires in this book are tools to help you find the best care. They are based on extensive research by the authors, who are experts in long-term care for older people. These quick and easy tools will help you know what to look for, how to judge quality, and how to make the best choices. Although other books contain lists of questions, none have been consistently tested and found to identify the quality of long-term care as have the questions in this book. For us, quality means getting the right care and services, at the right time, at the right place, at the right price, and provided by people who are knowledgeable, qualified, and caring.

This book will help you recognize high-quality assisted-living facilities and nursing homes. Some places are embracing new ideas such as the Eden Alternative, which emphasizes residents' quality of life and encourages them to bring pets, plants, and other homelike amenities into their rooms. Another positive trend is resident-centered care, in which residents make more of their own decisions and staff tailor care to individuals' needs. Greenhouses focus on homelike environments in small houselike settings. High-quality facilities are providing rehabilitation to help older people regain strength and skills so that they can return to independent living. They also provide encouragement and support to those who cannot return home, and offer holistic care to those who are terminally ill.

How to Find the Best Eldercare is based on the authors' more than three decades of experience and original research. We worked with numerous residents, families, and staff members of nursing homes and assisted-living facilities to develop walk-through observation guides. During tours of just twenty or thirty minutes, these guides help you evaluate the quality of care. The scoring guidelines help you rate each facility so that you can make a good decision based on the quality of care, the most important factor of all. The guides—one for assisted living and one for nursing homes—have been thoroughly field-tested in the United States and abroad.

In addition to the guides, we have included sets of questions you can use when interviewing staff as well as family members of residents in the places you visit. These questions come with a sort of "cheat sheet" providing the answers you would expect to hear in high-quality places.

To help you make the most of the answers you get and the observations you make, we describe high-quality care in assisted-living facilities and nursing homes, what in-home or senior housing long-term care options are available to consumers, how to finance long-term care, how to adjust to moving to senior housing or other new places, and where to find resources for more information and services.

To show what the decision-making process might be like, we have included one daughter's story—a true story—about her family's experience when her mother and mother-in-law needed in-home services, then assisted living, and eventually nursing home care. We hope this book will help relieve you of the guilt and fear that often accompany choosing long-term care, particularly assisted-living or nursing home care. We also hope that your experiences with long-term care will be as positive and life-affirming as possible.

CHAPTER ONE

Good News and Overwhelming News—Lots of Long-Term Care Options

The time comes for each of us. As we age, we eventually need assistance of some kind. We are fortunate to have many options for long-term care, but finding the best fit and high-quality services for yourself or your loved one can feel overwhelming. This book will help you through the process step by step.

To begin, what is long-term care and what are the options? *Long-term care* refers to a variety of services that help the person regain or maintain as much independence and health as possible for as long as possible. These services may last weeks, months, or even years. They could include anything from in-home services, such as help with shopping or preparing meals, to hospice care when faced with a terminal illness. Between those two extremes, long-term care could include housing options from apartments with housekeeping services to skilled nursing homes that provide rehabilitation or help with chronic illnesses.

You may be wondering, "How do I find a good homecare provider?" or "How do I find a good nursing home?" or "How do I find a good assisted-living facility?" or "How do I find good senior housing?" We help you find answers by providing questions to ask about a variety of service options. We have included easy-to-use guides for assisted-living facilities and nursing homes that allow you to evaluate such places in a twenty- to thirty-minute walk-through. We have carefully designed and tested the guides so that you can be sure they will give the information you need about quality care.

We also offer advice on how to adapt to life in any new type of housing, whether it's senior housing, assisted living, or a nursing home, and we suggest ways to finance care and locate resources locally and nationwide. The advice we've assembled here is based on years of experience working in and managing homecare, independent living, assisted living, and nursing homes. It's also based on research that we and other professionals have conducted on the quality of care in various settings—aging in place, assisted living, and nursing homes—and on conversations we've had with hundreds of long-term care staff members. Most important, we've learned about what is important from hundreds of individuals like you.

Before we get too far into this advice, though, let's cover some basics about long-term care and various service options you may want to consider for your care needs.

What are the options for long-term care?

When it comes to long-term care, nursing homes readily come to mind, but they are not the only option, and they may not be the best place for you or your loved one. Each person's needs are different, and it's important to consider every option.

Selecting the best option depends on many factors, such as whether someone is available for in-home assistance, how much personal and healthcare is needed, where you live, what community services are available, and your financial resources.

In addition to nursing homes, common long-term care options include senior services, homecare, hospice care, live-in help, independent senior housing with services, subsidized senior housing, board-and-care or group homes, assisted living (or residential care), and nursing homes. A brief description of each of these options follows.

Senior services

Contrary to what you might think, most assistance for seniors is not provided by government agencies, faith communities, or any formal group. Families, especially adult children, provide most of the help. They help with shopping, transportation, and personal care needs. Similarly, it is a myth that families abandon elders to nursing homes, which then provide most of the care. The truth is that for years before many elders enter assisted living or nursing homes, family and friends have volunteered a great deal of time to help.

If used wisely, senior services programs offered by various agencies can help delay the need to move to a long-term care center. Let's explore some options.

Senior centers offer meal programs to elders who can come to a meal site. For those who cannot attend, some communities offer a Meals on Wheels program. Senior centers may also offer social events, health-promotion screenings, and clinical services. Locate the nearest senior center by contacting your local Area Agency on Aging, asking local clergy, or contacting local public health agencies. The Internet is also a good source of information (see, for example, the Web site for the National Association of Area Agencies on Aging: www.n4a.org).

Many communities offer transportation to older adults who can no longer drive. This service is fundamental for helping people remain in their homes. Without it, many people could not get to the grocery store, to doctors' appointments, or to other important locations. Some communities transport people in wheelchairs, but many programs require that clients are able to walk to a van and get in and out with little assistance. Some programs charge fees, though costs are sometimes paid by public and private grants. Find out about these services through your local Area Agency on Aging, senior centers, clergy, public health agencies, and social services staff in local health clinics.

Adult daycare can be a good option for seniors who need help during the day but who have family to help them in the evening and at night. Some communities offer daytime programs that help seniors who can come to a location for activities, meals, and some personal assistance, such as bathing and help with the bathroom. This often allows family a respite from care to work and maintain other parts of their lives. Adult daycare generally works best when family members are willing to help, especially if the senior lives with the family. Such programs often specialize in caring for people with Alzheimer's disease or other kinds of dementia, or other long-term chronic illnesses requiring caregivers to help with daily activities like eating, bathing, or using the bathroom. Some states subsidize daycare services, so charges may be based on the ability to pay. Some private long-term care insurances cover the costs, and sometimes the senior or family pays.

Some communities offer private **case management,** or care coordination, through private companies or community service agencies. Case managers help seniors and their families find local services, coordinate medical care, and obtain financial assistance. Although seniors (or their families) must pay private case managers, they help people sort through long-term care options, arrange for services in their homes, and find assisted living or nursing home care. Some states pay for care management for those with financial need.

The Federal Older Americans Act established **Area Agencies on Aging** to coordinate funding for senior services and centers. The agencies also provide information about local services that help older adults remain healthy and independent in their own homes for as long as possible.

Various sources at federal, state, and local levels fund senior services. Even so, volunteers and fund-raising are essential to help these services meet the needs of their many clients who cannot afford all the services they need to remain in their homes. Working as a volunteer is a good way to figure out many of the options available in your community.

Homecare

After a hospitalization, many people hire a licensed homecare agency to help them recuperate at home. A nurse or physical therapist may come to the home to help manage the illness or to help the person regain mobility and strength. A nursing assistant may come to help with bathing and personal care. Generally, Medicare pays for some home health services for a limited time. Because Medicare home health is a federal program, licensed Medicare home health agencies exist nationwide.

To locate and compare the quality of nearby agencies, visit the national Web site www.medicare.gov. Under "Search Tools," click on "Compare Home Health Agencies in Your Area." This Web site lists quality care indicators so that each home health agency can be compared, if you have more than one choice in your community. Attention-worthy indicators include improvements in activities of daily living, healing of wounds, and rate of hospital readmittance. Another helpful Web site that lists all home health agencies is www.carepathways.com/homecare.cfm.

Some homecare services assist with housekeeping, shopping, and other household chores that are difficult for some older adults. Sometimes, a bit of weekly or daily service is enough to help someone manage their chronic illnesses while continuing to live at home.

Another valuable service can help manage healthcare issues and medications from multiple primary care providers. Medication management by a nurse care coordinator will likely help older people improve their health and continue living at home. Sometimes, local, county, or state programs pay for these services. Occasionally, private insurance pays, but often the individual or family must cover the costs.

Hospice care

At the end of life, special needs can be best handled by hospice staff educated for this work. Hospice services are available to anyone with a terminal illness. Hospice care costs are covered by Medicare, Medicaid, most private insurances, managed care organizations, and health maintenance organizations (HMOs). Anyone can contact a hospice and ask for services. Or, a physician can order services for a senior nearing the end of life. If health improves, the senior can resume pre-hospice care and return to the hospice later, if necessary.

Hospice services focus on providing comfort and care, not on curing illness. A hospice service will cover costs for primary care providers, nursing, medical equipment, medical supplies, drugs for controlling symptoms and relieving pain, homemaker and home health aide services, some therapy, dietary counseling, and grief support for seniors and family members. Hospice service is available for residents of long-term care facilities. Staff there can work closely with hospice staff to meet the senior's care needs.

It is really important for all people to have discussed end-of-life care options with family or a designated representative. Everyone should have an advance directive in place, which authorizes a person to make healthcare choices when the senior is unable to do so. Ask your healthcare provider for a copy of the advance directive forms for your state. You can also use the National Hospice and Palliative Care Organization's helpful Web site: www.caringinfo.org. This site also has advance directive forms that you can complete and give to your healthcare providers so that they know your wishes. Information about hospice services is also available at this site.

Live-in help

Some homecare agencies and other placement agencies will find workers to live with older adults and provide basic housekeeping, meal preparation, and assistance with personal care. The fee—paid by the day out of personal funds—is less than typical homecare, and the workers are available around the clock. The older adults provide the live-in person with meals, a bedroom, and the use of other space in the house.

When using this option, be sure that the agency is licensed, that employees have passed criminal background checks, and that they are trustworthy. Always get references. Either check the references yourself or have a trusted family member check them. Interview the person to be sure he or she is someone you like and trust. Ask other families who have used the agency about their experiences with the staff and their satisfaction with the services and payment process.

Independent senior housing with services

Some specially designed housing offers health and personal care services. Such housing is typically an apartment or condominium that includes conveniences to support independence, such as wheelchair-accessible bathrooms, showers, appliances, countertops, cabinets, power sources, and living spaces. Meals, activities, and transportation are usually part of the basic package. As residents develop more assistance needs, they can purchase assistance with personal care, medication supervision, care coordination, and other services from a licensed homecare agency or another provider. Personal funds pay for the housing, and most other services are paid by private insurance or personal funds.

Housing of this kind should be built to strict safety standards and have "universal access features." These features include ways to enter and exit living spaces without having to use steps; accessible toilet and shower areas with grab bars and no steps; and kitchen spaces in which elders can easily reach cabinets, water, and food.

Also, evaluate service options that include meals. Look for choices, and have a meal yourself to test the food. Talk to people who live in the housing development or friends and families of residents to learn about their experiences.

Subsidized senior housing

Federal and state programs subsidize housing for older and disabled adults with low and moderate incomes. In subsidized senior housing, residents generally live independently in an apartment within a senior housing complex. Many facilities encourage volunteer programs and activities that foster socializing. Some also offer assistance with shopping, laundry, or other tasks. Individuals may hire a homecare agency to help with healthcare or personal care needs; however, government funding usually will not cover the costs. As a person's care needs increase, nursing home placement becomes a viable alternative to the high cost of extensive in-home services.

To locate nearby subsidized senior housing, check with your local Area Agency on Aging, which maintains a list of federally approved subsidized senior housing. The agency can help you make contacts with housing managers. Typically, such housing has waiting lists, so it is important to get your name on the lists and move into an apartment when it becomes available. To evaluate the satisfaction of people who live in a housing development, meet the apartment manager and ask to speak with some tenants. Ask about their experiences. Also, be sure to evaluate the "universal access" and safety features of the building, as these are critical features.

Board-and-care or group homes

Board-and-care or group homes are community-based group living facilities designed for older adults who can no longer live independently. These homes typically are large private houses converted to accommodate eight to twenty people. Each person has his or her own bedroom. Residents share bathrooms, kitchens, living rooms, and porches, sometimes with the owner or operator. Most of these homes provide some assistance with bathing, walking, toilet use, and eating. Some states make public funding available for residents; otherwise, personal funds must cover the costs. As with assisted living, regulations may require transfer from board-and-care to a nursing home when a resident's care needs reach a designated point.

Tour the homes you are interested in, and use the assisted-living guide in chapter 4, pages 52–60, to measure quality of care. Most of that guide's items will apply to a board-and-care home. As always, talk to others who live in the home and meet with families of residents. They can tell you what it is like to live there.

Assisted living, residential care, community-based residential care

Assisted living, also called residential care or community-based residential care, is an increasingly popular option for older adults who need some help with personal care, such as bathing, meals, laundry, medications, and housekeeping. In assisted living, residents generally live in private apartments while sharing meals and activities with other residents.

Assisted-living facilities are not nursing homes. They provide less care and have fewer workers on staff. For example, in assisted-living facilities, registered nurses are rarely on duty around the clock, and rehabilitation therapists generally are not readily available, as they are in nursing homes.

If you or your loved one will need nursing care or rehabilitation therapy, ask about available services. A homecare agency may supplement the care the facility provides, but the senior will likely have to pay for homecare. In this case, a nursing home may be a more suitable, less costly option. In fact, some assisted-living facilities require residents to transfer to a nursing home if their care needs increase.

Licensing and funding vary from state to state, as do the definitions of residential care and assisted living. These facilities are often marketed to more affluent seniors, since personal funds usually pay for assisted living. However, some long-term care insurances may help with costs. Be sure to ask about the costs of medications and medication assistance, since residents usually must pay them.

Because more and more people are choosing assisted living, we have tested a quality-of-care guide for this setting to help you make a decision based on good quality of care. The guide in chapter 4, pages 98–101, helps you judge the quality of care and lists questions to ask residents and their families before moving in.

Nursing homes

Nursing homes are licensed to provide protective oversight of residents, as well as care and services that residents need when their physical or mental impairments prevent them from living independently. Some residents may need services for a short-term stay of a few weeks for rehabilitation and before returning home; others may stay for many months or years. Services include nursing care, nursing supervision, assistance with personal care, medical care, pharmacy services, medication administration, recreational activities, access to rehabilitation therapists and social workers, meals, and assistance with eating and laundry.

Most nursing homes in the United States are for-profit businesses. Some are owned and operated by not-for-profit organizations, such as faith communities, religious groups, fraternal groups, and other nonprofit agencies. A few are operated by governmental agencies, such as counties, districts, cities, or the Department of Veterans Affairs.

Nursing home care may be paid for through personal funds, private insurance, public assistance, or a combination of these. Typically, long-term nursing home residents pay for the first months or years of care with their personal funds. When these funds are depleted, the Medicaid program kicks in and pays for the care as long as the person lives. We discuss the financing of nursing home care in much more detail in chapter 5.

As we mentioned earlier, some residents stay only a short time. Medicare and other insurance usually pays for this care as a person rehabilitates from an illness or injury. Many nursing homes offer Medicare short-stay services, so this option is likely to be available in your community. Another service for short-stay rehabilitation is subacute rehabilitation, which is a more intensive level of rehabilitation. Hospitals or nearby affiliated facilities often offer this kind of care. A hospital social worker can help you determine whether a subacute rehabilitation unit or facility is available in your area.

The decision to move into a nursing home is a critical one. You will be much more satisfied traveling farther to a nursing home with good-quality care than settling for less in a place closer to where you live. Base your decision on quality of care rather than on appearance or location. This book offers tools to guide you and score the quality of care as you examine each facility carefully to determine which option is best for you. Find the guides for nursing homes in chapter 5, beginning on page 116. These guides will teach you how to look with a critical eye at the places where residents live, eat, enjoy life, and work on regaining or maintaining their health and well-being.

What long-term care options are available in my community?

Long-term care availability varies from community to community, and discovering the options will take some investigation. Start with agencies that advocate for older adults, such as your local Area Agency on Aging, senior center, healthcare organizations, community groups, department of social services, public health department, or library. For a helpful state-by-state list of resources, see chapter 7. Call and ask for guidance in obtaining listings of long-term care services. After just a few phone calls, you should have a good sense of what is available locally. When talking with long-term care providers, be sure to ask exactly what services are offered, what they cost, how to apply for them, and whether they are restricted in any way, such as by income, age, or disability. You will also want to ask whether financial assistance is available. We have prepared lists of questions for you to ask providers of senior housing in chapter 3, assisted living in chapter 4, and nursing homes in chapter 5. Also remember that the U.S. Social Security Administration may help if you qualify for Social Security benefits and Medicare.

How do I decide which long-term care option I need?

People need long-term care services for various reasons, but the overriding reason is that they need more help with activities of daily living, getting the right medication at the right time, managing multiple chronic illnesses like diabetes, heart problems, cancer, stroke, arthritis, and so on. We have prepared the following table to suggest which needs and services might go together, as well as which long-term care options might be appropriate.

Deciding on long-term care options

Basic Needs	Number of Basic Needs	Services to Consider
❐ Help with bathing ❐ Help with meal preparation ❐ Help with eating ❐ Help with walking ❐ Transportation to appointments ❐ Help with shopping ❐ Housekeeping ❐ Medication administration, assistance	For 1–2 basic needs, then consider →	Senior in-home services such as Meals on Wheels; help from a volunteer or family member; homecare service for chores or help; nursing care coordination
	For 2–4 basic needs, then consider →	Senior housing with services; live-in help
Additional Needs		
❐ Increasing health issues and/or some memory problems, severe vision or hearing problems	For 2–4 basic needs and these additional needs, then consider →	Assisted living
❐ Significant health issues like heart failure; disabilities from a stroke; hard- to-control blood sugars from diabetes; circulation problems in legs; difficulty breathing; incontinence; severe vision, hearing, or memory problems	For 4 or more basic needs and these additional needs, then consider →	Nursing home
❐ After hospitalization for intensive rehabilitation (physical, occupational, speech therapy) or restoration	For 4 or more basic needs and these additional needs, then consider →	Short-term Medicare nursing home or subacute rehabilitation

CHAPTER TWO

One Family's Story of Moving through Several Long-Term Care Options

Before we get into the specifics of how to judge the quality of a nursing home or assisted-living facility, we'd like to offer an example of one family's experience as they made decisions about long-term care and moved into both assisted living and a nursing home. Although every situation is unique, many families will share aspects of this experience. We have changed the names and locations, but the decisions and outcomes are very real. We include this story to reassure you that you are not alone in making these difficult choices, a task that continues as care needs change. But it is important to keep making decisions with the quality of care in mind. Another reason we include this story is to let you know that it really is okay to get help for yourself or your family member. Getting help is a loving thing to do.

A difficult decision

Nursing homes had always seemed like negative places to me. My first experience with one was when my Brownie troop visited the home of our leader's grandmother. We sang songs and gave the residents May baskets we had made. Even though we were doing a good thing and everyone was friendly and fussed over us because we were cute, we were frightened and glad to get out. I remember being told that it was a character-building event, that we would learn from it, and that the people who lived there were courageous and deserved our sympathy.

That was probably part of the reason why I took groups to nursing homes after I grew up and became a mom, a teacher, and a leader for lots of church-related activities. Usually we visited nursing homes to see elderly congregation members who were living there. My vacation Bible school classes visited to sing songs, recite verses, and put on puppet shows. We always received a lot of applause and cheers, and lots of cookies and juice.

I thought we were there to cheer up the residents, to brighten their dreary days. I felt sorry for the people who had to live in the nursing homes, and, most likely, without intending to, I communicated that feeling to my charges. No one I knew well actually lived in one. I was certain that nursing homes were terrible places, even though things looked all right when we were there. I knew I would never want anyone I loved to live there—certainly and especially not my mom.

But last summer, my husband and I did the unthinkable. After years of dealing with their declining health and growing dependence, we admitted both our beloved mothers to the same nursing home, one to a residential care unit, the other to skilled care. Circumstances made it necessary. It was hard on all of us, but it was the best thing we could have done—for Steve and me, for my father-in-law, for our children and grandchildren, and, most of all, for our mothers.

My mom

My mom has always faced health challenges. I grew up as an only child and I always worried about her, especially since my dad died when I was seven. Mom had to work, something most other moms didn't do at that time. I was a latchkey kid and was used to coming home to fix my own lunch. After I'd eaten, I would wash the dishes and read until it was time to return to school. I felt independent and resourceful. After school, however, it would be getting dark and my self-confidence would vanish with the daylight. I was always afraid that something terrible would happen to Mom on her way home from work—that a bus would careen around the corner and hit and kill her, or that someone would rob the bank next door to the newspaper office where she worked and shoot her. If she died, I'd be alone, really alone.

More often than not, though, my mom would be ill and have to stay home from work. Then I would eagerly come home at lunch and after school. Her illnesses ranged from viruses to pleurisy to female problems to heart problems. She'd tell me about the illnesses she'd had—about how she'd had rheumatic fever as a teenager and missed most of her junior year. She'd still graduated in the top five of her class, but her heart was permanently affected by the illness.

I worried about her all the time—when I went to pajama parties, when I went to camp, when I went on church youth trips, when I went away to college, and when I got married and moved four hundred miles away. When she retired from her newspaper job, she moved to the same city where Steve and I and our three children lived. She had a condo across town in a retirement community. There would be infrequent but disturbing emergencies, and I would go take care of her. Everyone but me understood that she would become "ill" whenever she wanted something or disapproved of something.

After our children graduated from high school and went to college, and after Steve received a promotion, we decided to move to a new community. We began building our dream house about forty miles south of where we were living. That was when Mom's illnesses became more frequent and severe. She disapproved of the move.

Her blood pressure, which had been kept in check for about twenty years by a daily pill, was now soaring to alarming heights. Every time her doctor gave her a new medicine, she became violently ill and would have to be taken to the emergency room.

By the time our new home was completed and our old home was sold, we realized that we would have to take her with us. She was always sick. Our new pastor told me that he thought she wanted to move in with us. I was resentful, but Steve wasn't surprised at all. We discussed the matter and knew that we did not want her to live with us, so we found her a duplex down the block from us.

Getting support services to help

As my mom's health—including her eyesight—worsened, she began to require more assistance at home. I set up as many programs as possible for her through our state's department of human services. One was a crisis line, a service that provided emergency aid for elderly people through our local hospital. This involved my mom wearing a small transmitter around her neck at all times. If she fell or needed help and could not get to a phone, she could press the button on the transmitter, signaling to an operator that she needed help. The hospital would then try to call Mom, and, if they couldn't reach her, they would call us or send an ambulance to her home.

Other helpful programs included our community's Meals on Wheels program, a service that Steve and I had worked with as volunteers through our church. Since Mom was losing her eyesight, a person from Lighthouse for the Blind would visit her once a month. She would assess Mom's needs and provide her with tools to help her in her daily life: a cooking timer with huge numbers, a powerful lamp, magnifiers, a talking watch, a special radio with a radio station for the vision-impaired, a four-track tape player for playing tapes of books, and a record player for playing recordings of magazines. These services were free.

Often, I hired friends, neighbors, and church members to help Mom. They would come in during the day while we were at work to check on her and stay with her if she were especially ill. We also hired someone to clean her apartment twice a month.

Steve's mother

My husband started looking at nursing homes for his mother at least a year and a half before I did. His mother has rheumatoid arthritis. She toughed it out for a long time, cleaning, cooking, and doing community work. But it was taking more and more time and more and more medication for her to accomplish these things.

Steve's mother had always taken care of her home and family. She was the world's greatest cook—at least her family, neighbors, and friends all thought so. Whenever someone was sick, she would make a huge pot of soup and a large loaf of bread to take to them. For every potluck, bake sale, or ham dinner, our church could always count on Mother. But as time went by, it became increasingly difficult for her to take care of things. Dad, who had always been the breadwinner, was puzzled and sometimes angry. He believed that she just wasn't trying hard enough.

Rheumatoid arthritis is a slow and horrifyingly progressive disease. Mother never complained; she didn't want to worry us, even when her condition worsened to the point that she couldn't walk on her own. Finally, she couldn't pick up a glass or fork, or comb her hair.

Steve came back from his nursing home searches depressed and angry. He spoke of the bad smells in the homes he had visited and the cries of the people who needed attention. Some workers were flush-faced and scurrying, overwhelmed by their responsibilities. Other employees were lethargic and appeared to ignore the people who needed assistance.

We worried about Dad. We feared that all of their money would go toward Mother's care, and that Dad would have nothing left for himself. Plus, Dad was demanding and had no idea how to cook or manage a home. We knew that it wouldn't work for Dad to live with us, or, for that matter, with any of Steve's brothers and sisters. It seemed wrong to feel this way, but we all agreed that this was so. All of us had jobs and families.

Finally, Steve found a good "senior housing facility." His dad could live in a supervised setting called assisted living. In the same complex was a nursing home where Steve's mother could stay. Dad would have his own room, his clothes would be washed, clean sheets and towels provided, and he could eat every meal with Mother and visit her as often as he wished. They could watch movies and eat popcorn together in the multipurpose room every Friday night. There would be card games and bingo several times a week; these were things they loved to do. There was one problem, however: Steve's parents refused to go. This was their home; this was where they would stay.

Their decision to stay home made it hard for everyone in Steve's family. We took turns washing clothes, cooking, and cleaning. Unfortunately, we also argued about who was doing the most for Mother and Dad. We'd never been this angry with each other before; we'd always been close. Some family members who had promised to do things didn't follow through. It was so hard for some of them to see Mother so crippled that they just wouldn't show up when it was their turn to help. And Steve's parents wouldn't "tattle" on them.

Steve's mother was receiving a few home services from Medicare: a social worker, a visiting nurse three times a week, a therapist once a week, and a bath lady three times a week. But they were there for only an hour at a time.

We were concerned about the times when no one but Dad was home with Mother. She couldn't walk to the bathroom. We found out from a neighbor that she would call and call for Dad to take her. He would either be asleep or ignore her, and she would end up wetting herself. She had sores that were becoming infected. She couldn't wipe herself after she went to the bathroom, and Dad refused to help her. He would not change her clothes, and she often wore the same outfit for days. We discovered that he was only feeding her one meal a day. He would go out for his meals—leaving her alone for an hour or more—and bring her back a sandwich.

Things weren't going well, but it took us a long time to understand that. We aren't stupid, ignorant, or cruel. We are nice, hardworking people. But as uncomfortable and unhappy as Mother was, she never complained. Both she and Dad told us they were doing fine. Only over time did it become apparent that Steve's mother would die if she didn't get better care.

Live-in help for Steve's mother

Steve investigated live-in homecare. We had heard good things about one agency from neighbors and acquaintances, and we decided to contract its services. Steve and his brothers and sisters cleaned out the spare bedroom so that the homecare worker would have a place to stay. We gathered stuff that had accumulated over decades, packed it in boxes, and stored it in the basement of our house.

Steve's mother was worried that their possessions would be lost or damaged. Dad was angry because he didn't want "some stranger" living in his house. Steve, as the eldest of his siblings, had to be the tough guy. Although it was difficult to do, he told his dad that Mother needed to be taken care of and that Dad hadn't been doing a good job of it. Because Dad had refused to go to the senior housing facility, we were going to have to get a live-in caregiver for Mother. Steve then said the words that would become the family's motto in the hard months and years ahead. "This isn't what you want, but it is what you need. We love you and we are going to do what you need, even if you get mad at us." Even now, Steve will shake his head and say, "I never thought I'd talk to my father that way." And even now, I must keep reminding him that we really are doing what they need.

We called the agency and hired a woman from Romania named Deanie, who stayed with Mother and Dad for about nine months. Deanie did a good job. She kept Mother clean, changed her clothes, gave her nutritious food to eat, made her do the exercises recommended by the visiting nurse and therapist, and got rid of her sores. But it was hard for Steve's parents to adjust to another person living in their house, and Deanie and Dad argued constantly. This was his home and his wife, and he knew what was best for Mother. But Deanie also wanted what was best for Mother; she was herself the mother of two sons and had formerly held an executive position in Romania. Deanie was used to giving orders. But she wasn't used to cooking, particularly American dishes. Dad hated her cooking.

Every two weeks, Steve or another family member would take Deanie to the train station so she could have two days off. During those two days, family members would take turns staying with Mother and Dad.

Taking care of Steve's mother was hard work, both physically and emotionally. Although Mother was a tiny woman, it was difficult to lift, dress, and wash her. Taking her to the toilet was strenuous, especially for the females in the family. Wiping and cleaning her was not a particular problem for the women and girls, but it provoked extreme discomfort in her sons. They did it anyway, because it was something that had to be done.

Because of Deanie, Mother gained weight, and her sores and infections healed. We knew that Dad and Deanie had some loud and bitter fights, but Mother was better off for Deanie being there. Eventually, however, Deanie decided to return to Romania, and the agency brought in a replacement named Sally.

Sally had been a math teacher in the country of Georgia, which was formerly a part of the Soviet Union. She was a widow with two grown sons. She told us that her sons were doctors but were having a hard time making enough money to support their families. Sally stayed for three months. She got along very well with Dad. She cooked the sort of food he liked, was an excellent caregiver for Mother, communicated well with the family, and, in her own quiet way, managed things quite well.

When Sally suddenly married a math professor from a nearby university, she sent her niece Marta in her place so that we wouldn't be left without someone to take care of Mother. But it quickly became apparent that Marta was not taking care of Mother as well as the two previous caregivers had. Mother's sores returned, and she complained that Marta would leave her for long periods of time to go for walks or drives in her car. Marta was not a good cook, and the dishes were left undone for long periods of time. The sinks, bathtub, and toilets were only cleaned every two weeks when a family member stayed over during Marta's days off. Mother had always been neat, and the messiness of the house disturbed her. We tried several times to get Dad and Mother to fire Marta—the agency would have provided a replacement on a day's notice—but they were used to her and refused to do it. Marta was by far the strongest caregiver they had had. She could pick Mother up and carry her with ease, something even her sons could not do.

My mom gets worse

In the meantime, my mom was having more health problems, the most debilitating being the loss of vision due to macular degeneration. Her blood pressure was out of control. My husband and I took turns staying with her. We often had to rush her to the emergency room in the middle of the night.

Because of the needs of our parents, Steve and I sometimes went days at a time without seeing each other. We were taking as much time off work as we could. Thankfully, the kids were grown, but one or the other of us was often unable to attend family gatherings because of the demands of providing care for our parents. On holidays, I usually stayed with my mother and didn't get to see the rest of the family. Mom was always ill; any small upset would send her blood pressure shooting up if I wasn't there to take care of her.

I often got only one to three hours of sleep a night. When I wasn't teaching, I was with my mom or taking care of my own house: cleaning, paying our bills, and sharing a few moments with Steve. I was drinking an alarming amount of coffee just to stay awake. As I look back, I realize how stressed and exhausted both Steve and I were as we struggled to care for our mothers.

Mom was hospitalized at Thanksgiving. After she was released, Medicare homecare workers began coming out to assist her. Like Steve's mother, Mom had a nurse, a physical therapist, a bath lady, and a social worker. She was also assigned an occupational therapist because of her decreasing eyesight. She was blind now except for a small area at the rim of her left eye. Then, just two weeks before Christmas, she developed sciatica. The sciatic nerve in her back was pinched, and she was in terrible pain. The doctor was careful about giving her pain pills because of her other medications. Through all of this, she kept insisting that she was independent and didn't want a stranger living in her apartment, and definitely did not want to go to a nursing home.

Holidays: More trouble

For years, Steve and I had hosted holiday dinners at our house, but my sisters-in-law took pity on us and said they'd host both Thanksgiving and Christmas that year. We were grateful; we couldn't have done it.

Probably the hardest day for me was Christmas. I had had the week before Christmas off from school. Even though I had been at Mom's house most of the time, Steve and I managed to decorate the house and wrap the presents. I had prepared several dishes to take to our family dinner (mostly in Mom's kitchen) and left them in our refrigerator. As usual, Steve and I had plans to set up some of the toys for our grandchildren to see as they entered the house. There's nothing like seeing their surprised, joyful, wondering little faces when they see the huge tree and all the presents! It's a grandma's dream.

Because Mom was sick, she refused to come to the family celebration or even over to our house for a short time. Even worse, she refused to let me attend. I did not get to watch my grandchildren discover their Christmas gifts. Steve called me on the phone, and, as he took pictures, I listened to my daughter describe what was happening. I stayed with Mom all day while everyone else, including Steve's parents, celebrated at his brother's house.

I was angry and ashamed that I hadn't been there when the kids arrived. I resented the fact that I had missed Christmas with the rest of our family. I had so looked forward to seeing my grandsons react to the toys we had set out in front of the Christmas tree. But I was a monster, wasn't I, to want that when my mom needed me?

Christmas crisis

Later that night, exhausted and emotionally drained, I left my mom sitting comfortably in her chair and came home to have a little bit of Christmas with Steve. I'd taken Mom to the bathroom, gotten her a drink, and told her not to move until I came back in a couple of hours.

Steve and I exchanged gifts, drank some eggnog, and fell asleep in front of the fireplace in each other's arms. We were awakened by the telephone. It was the crisis line calling to say that Mom had fallen at her duplex. It had been an hour and a half since I had left her. We raced over, got her up, and put her to bed. She had fallen on soft carpeting and was unharmed. Later, we learned that she may have had a mild stroke. I stayed with her until the day before New Year's Eve.

I was haunted by the fact that I had left Mom alone. I remembered how Marta had been leaving Steve's mother, and I felt that I was just as bad. Plus, lack of sleep and overwork were causing me to feel depressed and hopeless. I realize now that I was making unrealistic demands on myself. At the time, though, all I could think was that I was a monster, a bumbling, fumbling, inept monster who couldn't get anything right. I had to get some help. Maybe if someone else could take care of Mom, I could get some much-needed sleep, catch up on my work, get back to being close with my husband, and feel normal about myself again.

Live-in help for my mom

We called the same homecare agency that we had used for Steve's mother. The agency sent us a woman from Ukraine named Tara. I was so relieved. It was wonderful to have someone who knew how to take care of an elderly person. I gave Tara a list of phone numbers, baked a casserole, cleaned the apartment, and did everything else that I thought might help. Steve dragged me home and insisted that I go to bed. I slept pretty much straight through for two days. When I wasn't sleeping, I graded papers and made lesson plans. I called Mom two times a day.

Then one day Mom said that she was scared of Tara's gruffness. That same day, the visiting nurse came, discovered that Mom's blood pressure was sky-high, and strongly suggested that I fire Tara. I did, and, within hours, the agency sent Suzy, a woman from Poland, for an interview. Suzy appeared to be very competent. Unfortunately, Mom had a stroke after Suzy had been there for only two days. I was present when the stroke occurred. The bath assistant had just given Mom her shower and I was setting her hair. Suddenly the whole left side of her face drooped like it had melted; she tried to tell me that her hands were tingling, but only gibberish came out of her mouth. I immediately called 911. It was the day before school was scheduled to start. I stayed at the hospital all night. Then, because Mom was out of danger, I went to work the next day.

While Mom was hospitalized, we continued to pay Suzy. Friends would pick her up and take her to the hospital, where she kept Mom company during the day. Steve and I would visit Mom after work, then take Suzy back to Mom's apartment. Mom surprised the doctor and hospital staff by recovering very quickly. She was home in a week and a half, and Suzy took charge of her. Things were good. I got enough sleep, I could be at home, I could spend time with my husband, and I got to see other family members occasionally. We went to Mom's apartment twice a day, before and after work, to visit and to bring things they needed from the grocery store and pharmacy. On Suzy's days off, I stayed with Mom.

As was the case with Steve's parents, Mom's savings dwindled rapidly. In fact, hers would run out before theirs did. We needed to get Mom into a nursing home on private pay as soon as possible. When her money ran out, she'd be eligible for Medicaid. We wanted to place her quickly because we were afraid that it would be harder to get her into a nice home if she were already on Medicaid.

The nursing home search

We began again to look for nursing homes. But every time I visited one, I ended up crying in the administrator's office. How could I think of doing this? My mother, in a nursing home? All nursing homes are awful, aren't they?

Well, some of them are. I noticed many of the things that Steve had reported from his earlier research. The smells were the first clue that things weren't good. Also, the staff in many of the homes seemed overworked and overwhelmed.

But there were nice places, too—places where I could sense a genuine affection between the residents and workers. I encountered a nurse in one home patiently explaining to a resident about the change her doctor had made in her medicine. I saw workers and residents sharing a laugh together. I saw a resident hug an aide and call her "my girl" and "honey." I saw residents walking together arm in arm, one frail little woman helping another with poor eyesight to the dining room under the unobtrusive but watchful eye of an aide or nurse.

One of our nieces, who is a nurse, gave us a list of things to look for when we visited different nursing homes. This gave us definite, concrete signs to watch for, making the process less emotional and more rational.

The home we had looked at for Steve's parents was now full, so there was no room for my mom. Friends from church told us about a good home that was quite a bit farther away. We worried about placing my mom so far away, but we also wanted to get the best facility we could. We went to see it. It really was better than the one we had set our hopes on. She could have a room of her own. There were lots of activities. The people were kind. The place didn't smell.

We asked the employees how long they had worked there. We noticed that residents had a few pieces of their own furniture in their rooms, along with family pictures, afghans, stuffed animals, plants, and other homey things. Several people invited us into their rooms to look around, and they always ended up telling us about their family members in the pictures. We spent a lot of time talking to the people who lived there because we thought it was the best way to find out what the place was really like. We learned that we could bring the family dog and cat whenever we came to visit. Pets were not only allowed but encouraged, with the understandable exception that they couldn't be brought into the dining room. We found out which beauticians the residents preferred and what days were best for scheduling an appointment. We found out what soaps worked best in the whirlpool baths. We were told about church services, about the Friday night movies with popcorn, about the resident who gave occasional piano concerts, about the excellent laundry service. And everyone said the food was great, especially the raisin cream pie.

Explaining to my mom that it was time

We took Mom to visit the nursing home on Suzy's day off. Mom didn't like it, of course. We explained about her diminishing funds, and she countered with several different and impractical plans to keep her apartment. As lovingly as possible, and with many tears, I explained that we could no longer take care of her the way she needed to be taken care of. Our youngest daughter was planning to get married in September, and I needed time to do the million things that the mother of the bride must do. I couldn't prepare for the wedding, manage my home, teach school, and take care of Mom. We went ahead and made arrangements to move Mom to the home in June, the earliest that we could get her in.

Around the same time, Suzy announced that she would be leaving our employment in June. I felt that this was evidence of God's will. It was amazing to me that the day before Suzy planned to return to

Poland was the day Mom was scheduled to move to the nursing home. It helped me feel that we were doing the right thing; I was at peace with our decision.

Steve's mother: It's time, too

In the meantime, Steve's mother's sores were making her increasingly uncomfortable. A nurse we knew said that people could die from pressure sores if they became infected. That lit a fire under us. We went back to the home we'd chosen for my mother to ask about Steve's mother also becoming a resident. The floor she would need was filled except for a private room that cost fifteen dollars more a day. We said we would take it, with the understanding that Mother would be put into a semiprivate room as soon as one was available.

Living again

Both of our mothers are doing well. Since moving to the home, my mom's life has been saved several times. When her blood pressure goes up, the medical staff reacts immediately. A staff member told me that just last week my mom was talking with a brother and sister who were searching for a nursing home for their mother. She invited them into her room, told them why she had arranged the room as she had, and gave them advice about the beauty shop and food choices. She confided that she hadn't wanted to come to the home but that she now understood it was necessary. She probably never will tell me this, but I feel better knowing that she said it.

Steve's mother is being treated by a physical therapist for her arthritis. She has regained enough use of her hands that she can feed herself again. Her sores have healed, and she is beginning to take a few steps. Both of our mothers have made new friends. Dad is lonesome sometimes, but he is also free to visit with his friends more often. He comes to the nursing home to visit Mother and eat with her at least three times a week. We don't worry all the time, and our visits are pleasant. As before, some of Steve's family visit often; others make excuses. It isn't as necessary for all of us to take turns visiting, however, because we are not providing direct care for either woman. Now, professionals who know what they are doing are taking care of them.

I wish I could say that we had done everything right and that everything is perfect. But things are never perfect. Still, we did the best we could, and our mothers are now well taken care of. Our family squabbles less, and most important, we have our lives back again.

CHAPTER THREE

Senior Housing: Making a Good Decision

Most older adults prefer to remain in their own homes. But often an environment that is suitable for a growing family is not comfortable for seniors. Spacious two- and three-story houses that were great for youthful legs can become difficult as mobility or chronic health conditions make daily household chores challenging. That's when single-story living becomes preferable. Bathing and toileting facilities that are easy to access become priorities, as do convenient access to laundry appliances.

Many communities offer housing options that are specially designed for seniors. Federal accessibility standards are included in the apartments, and many have additional features designed by specialists. When touring senior housing, pay attention to these features, which we describe below. They are keys to making a good decision.

Universal access

The federal government publishes accessibility standards for facilities to follow when designing, building, and retrofitting senior housing, assisted living, and other such settings. These standards apply to both the exterior and interior of the building, as well as to parking lots and sidewalks. Walking surfaces should be flat, with no steps and surface changes that could cause tripping or difficulty for people using wheelchairs, walkers, canes, or other assistive devices. Accessible sinks are open underneath so that a person in a wheelchair can easily reach the sink and faucets. Toilet areas need to be large enough for transferring to the toilet with assistance and be of accessible height (taller than a typical toilet), and they must have grab bars. Kitchen cabinetry should be accessible without a step stool and have easy-to-open drawers and doors. Doorways should be a minimum of thirty-six inches wide, with lever openers or other devices to make them easy to open. These are just a few examples of the many regulations described at the Uniform Federal Accessibility Standards Web site (www.access-board.gov/ufas/ufas-html/ufas.htm).

Outdoor access

Most people want to come and go easily. Consider how easy it is to exit and enter apartments and the building for walking outdoors, shopping, or getting to community activities. Look at sidewalks and driveways: Are there curbs that will be a problem? Is there parking or a garage for a car? What about gardening—if this is a strong interest, are opportunities for this hobby available? And of course, consider how easy is it to exit the building in case of emergencies such as a fire.

Restrictions on pets or personal items

Some housing complexes encourage pets, but others restrict them. For the family dog, look for easy access to walking outdoors and make plans for how to clean up after the pet. If pets are allowed, there is often a required additional fee for each pet or charges for any pet damage.

Ask about any restrictions on personal items. The facility should provide a list of potentially hazardous items that may not be stored or used in apartments.

Meals and other services

In some cases, senior housing provides only housing. But other places offer services as part of the rental agreement or for an additional fee. These services may include meals, transportation to some appointments or outings, emergency call response, or health clinic services on-site. If such things are important to you, be sure to ask about them and get written descriptions with prices. Ask about price increases, which may occur annually or at some regular interval.

Nurse-managed health clinics are becoming popular in senior housing. These services can help seniors delay or avoid nursing home care by staying healthier longer. Our studies of these services found that nurse-managed clinics in senior housing are remarkably helpful. The nurses get to know the residents well and can detect when they are getting ill. The nurses help elders get the healthcare services they need so that they can recover quicker and regain their strength and mobility faster. Ask if a nurse-managed health clinic is available in the senior housing you are considering.

Emergency response programs may include an emergency call system in bathrooms and bedrooms. Ask about who will respond in an emergency. There may be an apartment manager who responds, or it could be another worker. If emergency calls are frequent, it may be best to look at other services or settings, such as assisted living, to better ensure this type of care.

Independent senior housing with services

Some specially designed housing facilities offer health and personal care services in addition to apartment-style living. Typically, this type of housing is part of an apartment or condominium development with features that support independence, such as wheelchair access to bathrooms, showers, cabinets, and power sources; accessible kitchen spaces for cabinets, water, food, and laundry; and other specially designed living spaces.

Meals, activities, weekly housekeeping, and transportation are usually part of the basic service package. Unlike most traditional senior housing, as healthcare needs develop, residents can purchase assistance with personal care, medication supervision, care coordination, and other services from a licensed homecare agency or another provider. Personal funds pay for the housing; most other services are paid with private insurance or personal funds.

Carefully evaluate service options that include meals. Look for choices and have a meal to assess the food yourself. Talk to residents or family members associated with the housing development about the quality of the service options. Be sure to ask about emergency response. In particular, ask who will respond, and whether someone is available to respond twenty-four hours every day.

Subsidized senior housing

Federal and state programs subsidize housing for older and disabled adults with low and moderate incomes. In subsidized senior housing, residents generally live independently in an apartment within a senior housing complex. Many facilities encourage volunteer programs and social activities. Some also offer assistance with shopping, laundry, and other tasks. Individuals may hire a homecare agency to help with healthcare or personal care needs; however, federal, state, and local funding usually will not cover the cost of these services. As an individual's care needs increase, nursing home placement becomes a viable alternative to the high cost of extensive in-home services.

To locate subsidized senior housing in your community, contact your local Area Agency on Aging, which maintains a list of federally approved subsidized senior housing locations and can help you make contact with housing manager. Typically, such places have waiting lists, so get your name on the list early and be prepared to move into an apartment when it becomes available.

To evaluate the satisfaction of people who live in a housing development, meet the apartment manager and ask to speak with some tenants. Ask about their experiences and satisfaction. Also, be sure to evaluate the universal access and safety features of the building, as these are critical.

Evaluation of senior housing

Call and make appointments with the housing managers to tour the grounds and apartment buildings. As you approach the building, take note of the neighborhood, grounds, and parking.

Because a tour is your best opportunity to evaluate a senior housing building, you need to know exactly what to look for during the walk-through. On pages 38–40, you will find a detailed questionnaire indicating what to watch for and ask about. Make as many copies of this questionnaire as you need, and take a copy along on every tour. Take notes as you ask questions and make observations. We have also prepared a summary sheet for comparing senior housing on page 37. After visiting several facilities, you can use your summary sheet notes and questionnaires to make a good decision.

Many Web sites provide resources to help evaluate senior housing. The following are some particularly useful sites:

- www.aoa.gov/eldfam/Housing/Independent_Living/Senior_Apts.aspx
- www.calregistry.com/housing/srapts.htm
- www.seniorresource.com/hsoa.htm
- www.aaacap.org/seniornetwork.html

Key points to remember when choosing senior housing

- Are indoor and outdoor walkways flat, without steps or curbs?
- Do bathrooms have grab bars, step-in showers, and accessible sinks?
- Is lighting good, with natural light and easy-to-use lights and lamps?
- Are the services you want provided, such as housekeeping, meals, etc.?
- Are security and emergency response available?
- Are there social activities of interest, and friends and family nearby?

Summary sheet for comparing senior housing

Facility	Location	Contact Information	Visit Date	Notes

Senior housing walk-through questions

Facility ______________________ Date __________ Time __________

Things to look for and questions to ask when visiting senior housing:

Outdoors

- Are the building and grounds maintained?
- Are sidewalks and driveways clear for coming and going to the building?
- Are curbs modified so wheelchairs can access all sidewalks and driveways?
- Is there convenient parking for visitors?
- Is parking available for people living in the apartments? Is there a charge for parking?
- Is covered or garage parking available? Is there a charge?
- Is there lighting around the outside of the building, particularly around parking?
- Are there areas for walking?
- Are there areas for gardening?
- Are there outdoor spaces that could be enjoyed in good weather?
- Are the grounds of the building secured?
- Is the building locked at night? Who has keys?
- Is there a security person in the building at night?
- Are other staff members in the building twenty-four hours a day? If not, when are staff in the building?
- What about shopping? Are there stores nearby?

- What about community events and places of worship? Are those nearby?
- Ask residents if they spend time outdoors.

Apartments and common living spaces

- Are there any steps or stairs?
- Are the floor surfaces easy to walk on? Are they clean?
- Are interior halls well lighted?
- Are common spaces well lighted, and do they have some natural light?
- If meals are provided, how far is the walk to the dining room? Will that distance be accessible?
- Is the apartment lighted adequately?
- Are there windows providing natural light?
- What kitchen appliances are provided?
- Does each apartment have a washer and dryer? If not, can they be installed?
- Is the bathroom space large enough for safe use, particularly for a walker or wheelchair?
- Is the shower easy to walk into or step into?
- Do showers and toilets have grab bars?
- Can you easily reach the sink in the bathroom? Is it easily accessible from a walker or wheelchair?
- Are the cabinets and sink accessible in the kitchen?
- Is there adequate cabinet and closet storage?
- Is other storage available? Are there fees for additional storage?
- Ask residents what they like about their apartments and the building.

Costs and services

- Is a deposit required?
- What is the monthly rent?
- Are rent subsidies available for residents? If so, what is the procedure for approval?
- Are heating and electricity costs included in the rent?
- Are telephone, cable television, and Internet access available? At what charges?
- Is there a common laundry room with washers and dryers available? At what cost?
- Are meals provided? At what cost?
- Is transportation provided? At what cost?
- Is public transportation available? If so, how can it be accessed?
- Are pull cords or push buttons available in apartments for emergencies?
- Is emergency response available? Who will respond? Are there additional fees for using the emergency response?
- Are pets allowed? Are there additional charges for pets?
- Is there a health clinic on-site? Does a nurse manage it? Are there charges?
- Are personal services such as bathing assistance or other assistance available? At what cost?
- Are hospitals and health clinics nearby?

CHAPTER FOUR

Assisted Living: Making a Decision about Quality of Care and Services

Assisted-living facilities have become common in the past twenty years. These facilities can help older adults who need some assistance with personal care, bathing, meals, laundry, medications, housekeeping, and other activities. Many seniors find assisted living more appealing than nursing homes: residents generally live more independently in private apartments while sharing meals and activities with other residents, and the facilities are generally smaller and more homelike.

Assisted-living facilities are different from nursing homes in other ways. They provide less care, and their staff is usually smaller and includes fewer professional nurses. Typically, registered nurses or licensed practical nurses are not on duty around the clock, and rehabilitation therapists may not be readily available. Ask for more information about the availability of these services. Some assisted-living facilities have supplemental arrangements with homecare agencies, but you will likely have to pay for such services. Compare the costs of assisted living with additional services to the costs of local nursing homes. A nursing home may be less costly and provide more of the services you want. Be sure to ask about situations that may require a resident in assisted living to transfer to a nursing home. This can happen if the need for care increases.

People pay the costs of assisted living primarily from personal funds. Check with your state government—some states offer public funding, including Medicaid, to help those in need. Assisted-living facilities do not participate in Medicare. Be sure to discuss payment options and have a clear idea of the situations that may require transfer to a nursing home and what payment options will be needed if that occurs. On average, assisted living costs about $2,000 to $4,000 a month, depending upon the living space and services provided.

Board-and-care homes are one type of assisted living. These facilities can range in size from very small (serving one to six residents) to large facilities serving more than a hundred people. They generally offer some assistance with dressing, grooming, bathing, meals, housekeeping, and laundry. Healthcare services are generally not provided, so it's not a good choice for people who need daily nursing care or supervision. Costs for board-and-care homes range from $350 to $3,500 a month, depending on the services and the living space provided.

How do I evaluate the quality of assisted living?

We have written and tested questions that you can use in searching for good-quality assisted living. Even the best location will not work for you in the long run unless the care is good. Many features go into quality assisted living. Our research found that consumers want homelike surroundings, caring staff members who help residents with their care needs, accessibility, choices of things to do and places to go, good food, good lighting, appealing and accessible outdoor spaces, and the ability to have pets and plants if they want them.

We will explain these features and look at the walk-through guide we prepared and tested for assisted living on pages 52–60.

Homelike surroundings

An assisted-living facility should feel and look homelike. The common spaces should be appealing, like a living room where you could visit comfortably with a friend. Ask to see a resident's room or apartment. You should see a space that is personalized with furniture, pictures, and other things that have meaning to the person living there. If the resident is there, greet him or her and ask how he or she likes the apartment and living there.

Notice any odors. If you smell urine or feces, it likely indicates problems with the care. If you notice these odors, continue your search for good assisted-living facilities. If there are no odors, observe the cleanliness of the environment, residents, and staff. The environment should be clean and uncluttered, and residents and staff should be clean and well groomed. These are signs of good quality care.

Caring and care needs

Watch how comfortable the residents are with the staff. You should have the sense that residents and staff are caring, friendly, and kind to each other. You should see residents walking and moving about the facility. There should be a feeling of life and activity.

Most residents seek assisted-living services because they need some help with bathing or other personal care, medications, or help with managing chronic health conditions. One of the major limitations of assisted living is that as care needs increase, state regulations require residents to move from assisted living to a nursing home. It will help if you plan for this move, should the need arise or if care needs are likely to increase.

Access and choice

At home, we typically can reach for food and drink any time of the day or night, and the same should be true for assisted living. Look for this sort of access. Choices for meals are also important. Ask about menu choices and whether family members can join residents for meals.

Because many people value social activities, assisted-living facilities should offer events and activities that involve residents and staff. Check out whatever activities are happening during your tour and look for a calendar listing routine activities. Also, since many families stay connected by telephone, video phone, and e-mail, investigate access to the appropriate equipment and services.

Regular access to nurses is key to staying healthy in assisted-living facilities. Facilities with good-quality care have a nurse on staff and in the facility routinely—as much as daily. At other times, a nurse should be on call. The nurse may be a registered nurse (RN) or licensed practical or vocational nurse (LPN or LVN). Our research has found that when an RN visits residents a few times a week, they can offer advice to help residents stay healthy. And when residents are ill, nursing know-how helps them get the healthcare they need promptly so that they recover more quickly. This sort of care from an RN who knows the residents well helps many seniors avoid or delay a move to a nursing home.

Federal regulations for providers have not set staffing requirements for assisted living, so you will find staffing differences among assisted-living facilities. But some basic principles can help you decide whether staffing is adequate. For starters, there should be enough nursing assistants available so that all residents can get the care they need, be clean and dressed, and enjoy life. Staff should care for the same residents routinely to get to know them well and ensure they get the care and services they want and need. The staff should include licensed nurses who know the residents well.

Nursing homes require certified nursing assistants (CNAs) on staff. In assisted-living environments, nursing assistant staff may be CNAs or personal care assistants who are trained by the organization. Additionally, all staff in healthcare should have criminal background checks before hire, but that may not be required in some states. Be sure that a facility you are interested in performs background checks on potential staff members.

Access to an emergency call system is also important. Emergency call pull cords are located in bathroom and bedroom areas. This is different from the typical hospital and nursing home call-button for summoning staff for a variety of reasons from small requests to emergencies. In assisted living, emergency pull cords are only used in true emergency situations.

In assisted-living settings, residents usually need to make their own clinic appointments with their healthcare provider. Ask about transportation to clinic visits. In contrast, physicians and other healthcare providers typically come to nursing homes, rather than requiring residents to come to their clinic.

Lighting

Look for good lighting in residents' rooms and in common spaces. Natural lighting brightens daytime routines, and properly arranged electrical lighting makes for pleasant evening activities, such as reading.

Pets and plants

Before coming to assisted living, many residents enjoyed living with family pets. That can continue in assisted living. Many assisted-living facilities encourage residents to have a pet or share one with other residents. Look for pets and plants on your visits to assisted-living facilities, and ask if pets are allowed to visit or live there. When you see pets and plants in a facility, notice if they appear well cared for. That is important, too.

Outdoor spaces

Most people enjoy some time outdoors. Facilities should offer inviting outdoor areas. Look for shade and shelter for warm-weather and cool-weather comfort.

Universal access

Just as in senior housing, assisted-living facilities should follow federal accessibility standards when designing, constructing, and retrofitting their buildings. These standards apply both to the exterior and interior of the building, as well as to parking lots and sidewalks. Walking surfaces should be flat, with no steps or surface changes that could cause tripping or difficulty for people using wheelchairs, walkers, canes, or other assistive devices. Accessible sinks are open underneath so that a person in a wheelchair can easily reach the sink and faucets. Toilet areas need to be large enough for transferring to the toilet with assistance and be of accessible height (taller than a typical toilet) with grab bars. Kitchen cabinetry should be accessible without a step stool and have easy-to-open drawers and doors. Doorways should be a minimum of thirty-six inches wide, with lever openers or other devices to make them easy to open. These are just a few examples of the many standards specified at the Uniform Federal Accessibility Standards Web site (www.access-board.gov/ufas/ufas-html/ufas.htm).

Government inspections

Each state licenses and inspects assisted-living facilities and makes the results available upon request. Some inspection reports are posted on the World Wide Web. Ask about the results when touring facilities. The state license should be on display, and staff should be able to give you a copy of the latest state inspection report when asked. This is a good way to get an overview of any problems the facility may have had in complying with requirements, including safety guidelines.

Inspection results are just one way to look at the quality of care in assisted living. The real test is to inspect the facility yourself and look for the key signs of quality care. To make this task easy and productive, we've created a guide that defines what you should look for, how you should rate what you see, and what questions you should ask. We've also included the kinds of answers you'll hear at good facilities. Find the guide on pages 62–68. We even provide evaluation forms that you can photocopy and take with you when touring different facilities. Using this guide, you will be able to walk through any assisted-living facility and rate its quality of care in thirty minutes or less.

Helpful Web sites with information about assisted living include:

- www.helpguide.org/elder/board_care_homes_seniors_residential.htm
- www.alfa.org/i4a/pages/index.cfm?pageid=3278
- www.aahsa.org/article.aspx?id=3784
- www.bjbc.org/page.asp?pgID=209
- www.aarp.org/families/housing_choices
- www.ltcombudsman.org/static_pages/ombudsmen.cfm

The walk-through

The next step is to visit facilities and look for the six signs of quality we mentioned earlier: homelike setting, caring environment, access and choice of services, plants and pets, and outdoor spaces. Selecting a facility is a difficult and important task, so be prepared to shop around. Plan to visit several facilities before making a decision. As you look, remember that you are searching for the best care possible.

Start by visiting assisted-living facilities in your community—you may find that the best one is close to home. Convenience is great, however, but if you are not satisfied with local facilities, keep looking. It is better to find a good facility farther from your home than settle for substandard care close by. We have talked to many families who agree.

When considering a facility, call and make an appointment to take a tour. In most small assisted-living facilities, the administrator handles admissions. Or, you could start by simply going to the facility to observe and talk with some of the staff. When you are ready, explain to a staff member that you are looking for an assisted-living facility and ask if they can give you a tour.

Taking a tour is your best chance to evaluate a facility, so make the most of the opportunity. Beginning on page 52, you will find a detailed questionnaire to guide you; advice on what you should see and experience begins on page 62. These materials tell you specifically what to watch for and how to judge quality of care. Make as many copies of this questionnaire as you need, and take a copy along on every tour. Then, after visiting several facilities, review and compare your notes.

We based the walk-through questions on years of research with consumers and providers of assisted-living care. The questionnaire has been tested in more than 250 assisted-living facilities, so we're confident that it will help you in your search.

Before answering the walk-through questions, we recommend that you tour the facility for a few minutes during general business hours (between 10 a.m. and 6 p.m.). Walk through common living spaces, hallways, and other areas that are generally open to the public. Ask yourself, "Is this a place where I would feel comfortable living?" Be a good observer; think about what you see, hear, smell, and feel. Listen to your senses and trust your judgment.

A note about choosing your answers: The multiple-choice answers range from 1 to 5, with 1 indicating the worst quality of care and 5 indicating the best. Be sure to answer every question that applies to that facility. If you have difficulty scoring a particular question, you may need to walk through some areas a second time. To answer certain questions, you may need to ask staff about the care and services (questions 22, 23, 24, 27, and 28).

For best results, add the scores for all the questions to get a total. This "quality score" will range from 34 to 170. A score of 34 indicates the lowest quality of care; 170 indicates the highest. Our research shows that scores of 151 or more indicate a good-quality assisted-living facility. Homes scoring 116 or less indicate quality problems, so keep looking. Scores between 116 and 151 are typical of most facilities. The higher the score, the more likely you are to be satisfied with the care and services, so make sure you have found the best available in your area. Driving a bit farther for good care is worth it in the long run.

We know from our research that the questionnaire works best if you take the tour with a friend or family member who also scores the facility. Don't talk to each other about your answers until you have both answered all questions. Then talk about what you saw and take the average of both of the scores for each question.

After touring several facilities, go to the summary sheet on page 51, and compare quality scores and other pertinent information before choosing a facility.

The assisted-living tour is only part of your evaluation. Interview staff members and talk to families with loved ones living in that facility. Ask them questions from the guides on pages 83–93 and 98–101. Together, the three questionnaires will give you a complete picture of life in a particular facility.

Key points to remember when choosing an assisted-living facility

- Residents should be clean, groomed, dressed, up and about, and involved in indoor and outdoor activities.
- Staff members should be clean, groomed, friendly, active, helpful, and, most important, caring.
- Interaction between staff members and residents should be friendly and relaxed. Both staff members and residents should treat each other with respect and dignity.
- Facilities should be clean, uncluttered, well maintained, and well lighted.
- There should be no unpleasant odors, such as urine.
- The atmosphere should be calm, pleasant, homelike, and full of life.
- There should be a variety of activities and good food to enjoy.

Summary sheet for comparing assisted-living facilities

Facility	Location	Contact Information	Visit Date	Quality Score	Notes

Assisted-living walk-through questions

Facility ______________________ Date ____________ Time ____________

1. Were residents dressed and clean?

1	2	3	4	5
Most were not	*Some were*	*Many were*	*Most were*	*All were*

2. Were residents well groomed (shaved, hair combed, nails clean and trimmed)?

1	2	3	4	5
Most were not	*Some were*	*Many were*	*Most were*	*All were*

3. Did the facility seem calm?

1	2	3	4	5
Very chaotic	*Somewhat chaotic*	*Calm at times*	*Frequently calm*	*Calm most of the time*

4. Was there a pleasant atmosphere or feeling about the facility?

1	2	3	4	5
Very unpleasant	*Somewhat unpleasant*	*More or less pleasant*	*Quite pleasant*	*Very pleasant*

5. Were residents' rooms personalized with furniture, pictures, and other things from their past?

1	2	3	4	5
Most were not	*A few were*	*Some were*	*Many were*	*Most were*

6. Was there a homelike appearance or feeling about the facility?

1	2	3	4	5
Not at all homelike	*Somewhat*	*Moderately*	*Quite homelike*	*Very homelike*

7. Were hallways and common areas uncluttered?

1	2	3	4	5
Very cluttered	*Frequently cluttered*	*Somewhat cluttered*	*Neat and uncluttered*	*Very neat and uncluttered*

8. Were resident rooms, hallways, and common areas clean?

1	2	3	4	5
Dirty	*Somewhat dirty*	*More or less clean*	*Clean*	*Very clean*

9. Were buildings, grounds, and furniture in good condition?

1	2	3	4	5
Very poor condition	*Poor condition*	*Fairly good condition*	*Good condition*	*Very good condition*

10. Were loud or disturbing noises noticeable in the facility?

1	2	3	4	5
Pervasive throughout	*In most areas*	*Occasionally*	*Hardly at all*	*Not at all*

11. Were odors of urine or feces noticeable in the facility?

1	2	3	4	5
Pervasive throughout	*In most areas*	*Occasionally*	*Hardly at all*	*Not at all*

12. Were other unpleasant odors noticeable in the facility?

1	2	3	4	5
Pervasive throughout	*In most areas*	*Occasionally*	*Hardly at all*	*Not at all*

13. Were the conversations between staff and residents friendly?

1	2	3	4	5
Most were not	*A few were*	*Some were*	*Many were*	*Most were*

14. Did staff call residents by name?

1	2	3	4	5
Rarely seen	*Occasionally*	*Sometimes*	*Often*	*Very often*

15. Were interactions between staff and residents comfortable (for example, smiles, eye contact, touch, etc.)?

1	2	3	4	5
Most were not	*A few were*	*Some were*	*Many were*	*Most were*

16. Were interactions between staff and residents positive (for example, conversation, humor, touch, eye contact, etc.)?

1	2	3	4	5
Most were not	*A few were*	*Some were*	*Many were*	*Most were*

17. Were staff visible?

1	2	3	4	5
Rarely seen	*Occasionally*	*Sometimes*	*Often*	*Very often*

18. Did staff appear caring (compassionate, warm, kind)?

1	2	3	4	5
Most did not	*Some did*	*Many did*	*Most did*	*All did*

19. Did staff treat residents as individuals with dignity and respect?

1	2	3	4	5
Most did not	*Some did*	*Many did*	*Most did*	*All did*

20. Were residents walking or independently moving about the facility with or without assistive devices such as canes, walkers, or wheelchairs?

1	2	3	4	5
Rarely seen	*Occasionally*	*Sometimes*	*Often*	*Very often*

21. Was there a feeling of life and activity about the facility?

1	2	3	4	5
Not at all alive	*Somewhat alive*	*Moderately alive*	*Quite alive*	*Very much alive*

22. How often is a nurse (RN or LPN) present in the facility? (May need to ask staff.)

1	2	3	4	5
Monthly	*Biweekly*	*Weekly*	*Twice a week*	*Daily*

23. Did residents have a variety of foods to choose from at mealtime? (Look for posted meal plans; may need to ask staff.)

1	2	3	4	5
No choices	*Few*	*Some*	*Many choices*	*Very many choices*

24. Did residents have access to snacks and other foods at any time? (Look for posted signs about access to snacks; may need to ask staff.)

1	2	3	4	5
No access	*Rarely*	*Occasionally*	*Often*	*Access at all times*

25. Were a variety of activities available for residents? (Look for posted schedules, calendars, group meetings, etc.)

1	2	3	4	5
Rarely seen	*A few were*	*Some were*	*Many were*	*Lots were*

26. Were there activities involving children? (Look for posted activity schedules, calendars.)

1	2	3	4	5
None seen	*Occasionally*	*Sometimes*	*Often*	*Very often*

27. Did residents have access to telephone communication? (May need to ask staff.)

1	2	3	4	5
No access	*Rarely*	*Occasionally*	*Often*	*Access at all times*

28. Did residents have access to e-mail or other computer-based communication? (May need to ask staff.)

1	2	3	4	5
No access	*Rarely*	*Occasionally*	*Often*	*Access at all times*

29. Were the hallways well lighted?

1	2	3	4	5
Poorly lighted	*Some light but not enough*	*Moderately lighted*	*Well lighted*	*Exceptionally well lighted*

30. Were the common areas well lighted?

1	2	3	4	5
Poorly lighted	*Some light but not enough*	*Moderately lighted*	*Well lighted*	*Exceptionally well lighted*

31. Were there pets (dogs, cats, birds, etc.) and/or live plants in the facility?

1	2	3	4	5
None or rarely seen	*Occasionally*	*Sometimes*	*Often*	*Very often*

32. Were the pets and/or live plants in good condition?

1	2	3	4	5
None seen or poor condition	*Fair condition*	*Average condition*	*Good condition*	*Very good condition*

33. Were there outdoor gardens or other outdoor spaces for residents to enjoy?

1	2	3	4	5
None seen	*Very few*	*More or less*	*Some*	*Many spaces*

34. Did residents have access to outdoor spaces?

1	2	3	4	5
No apparent access	*Occasional access with assistance*	*Some access with assistance*	*Frequent access*	*Access any time*

Add the scores from all thirty-four questions to get a total score. If two persons completed the questionnaire, add the scores together and divide them by two. The average total score is the most accurate "quality score." A score of 151 or higher suggests a good-quality assisted-living facility. A score of 116 or lower suggests a facility with problems. Scores between these numbers are typical of most assisted-living facilities. The higher the score, the more likely you are to be satisfied with the care and services, so make sure you have found the best you can find in your area. Keep looking. Driving a bit farther for good care is worth it in the long run.

Note: This Questionnaire is officially titled "OBSERVABLE INDICATORS OF NURSING HOME CARE QUALITY" ASSISTED LIVING/ RESIDENTIAL CARE VERSION 10AL (Revised – June 2006) MU MDS and Quality Research Team © 1999, 2000, 2002, 2005, 2006.

User's guide to walk-through questions for assisted-living facilities

The following is a user's guide to explain the questions and how to judge your answers to each of the thirty-four walk-through questions for assisted-living facilities.

1. Were residents dressed and clean?

2. Were residents well groomed (shaved, hair combed, nails clean and trimmed)?
   Appearance is important to all of us, regardless of our age. Residents should appear well groomed, clean, and dressed appropriately for what they are doing and the time of day. Most assisted-living residents dress and groom themselves independently.

3. Did the facility seem calm?
   What is the demeanor or mood of the staff and residents? Do staff members appear frantic, disorganized, or hurried as they move about, or do they perform their work in a calm manner?

4. Was there a pleasant atmosphere or feeling about the facility?
   Would you want to spend time in this place? Trust your feelings.

5. Were residents' rooms personalized with furniture, pictures, and other things from their past?
   It is important that residents have personal items, because this is their home now.

6. Was there a homelike appearance or feeling about the facility?
   The facility should look and feel like a home, not an institution. Residents should live, not just reside. Do you think residents can enjoy the facility and feel good about it? If you had a family member in the facility, would you like to come here often? If you were a resident, would you be comfortable?

7. Were hallways and common areas uncluttered?
   Because assisted-living facilities are busy places with lots of people living and working in them, some clutter is likely. However, it should not be hazardous to walk or to wheel a wheelchair throughout the facility.

8. Were resident rooms, hallways, and common areas clean?
   They should be clean, that is, free from dust, mold, mildew, stains on the floors or walls, etc. Floors should be clean but they do not have to be shiny, because people with vision problems may struggle with glare on floors.

9. Were buildings, grounds, and furniture in good condition?
   This is home. The building, grounds, and furniture should be in good condition. Residents should feel safe and take pride in their surroundings.

10. Were loud or disturbing noises noticeable in the facility?
    Since loud noises are disturbing to everyone, you should not be overwhelmed by the noise level in the facility. Are employees talking loudly outside residents' rooms? Are televisions or radios being played loudly? Do the employees talk to each other in loud voices or by yelling? At times a facility may seem loud and chaotic. Generally, however, the facility should seem calm and be free from loud or disturbing noises.

11. Were odors of urine or feces noticeable in the facility?
    These odors should not be pervasive in the facility any more than they would be in your home. If there is a strong odor of urine or feces, it likely indicates major problems with the quality of care.

12. Were other unpleasant odors noticeable in the facility?
    When personal hygiene of residents is poor or when housekeeping or maintenance is inadequate, unpleasant odors become apparent. This should not be the case.

13. Were the conversations between staff and residents friendly?
    It is important that staff know the residents and communicate in a friendly manner. Did you observe staff talking to the residents about things other than resident care? For example, did the conversation focus only on medications or symptoms? Or did they also discuss family, friends, the weather, and other non-care-related topics?

14. Did staff call residents by name?
    Staff and residents should be friends, and calling one another by name indicates a friendly relationship. Staff need to know residents well enough to recognize when they are not behaving normally, which may indicate an illness.

15. Were interactions between staff and residents comfortable (for example, smiles, eye contact, touch, etc.)?

16. Were interactions between staff and residents positive (for example, conversation, humor, touch, eye contact, etc.)?
    Friendly nonverbal communication—for example, smiling, making eye contact, touching, etc.—is as important as good verbal communication. Residents and staff need to be comfortable with each other. Because they interact daily, nonverbal clues can tell you a lot about how people relate. As we mentioned earlier, those friendly relations help residents stay healthy.

17. Were staff visible?
    As you tour the facility, you should see staff members working throughout the place. It is important that staff be around to help residents with scheduled and unscheduled needs.

18. Did staff appear caring (compassionate, warm, kind)?

19. Did staff treat residents as individuals with dignity and respect?
    Although each staff member cares for several residents, they need to know the residents and treat them as individuals with their own needs and as people worthy of their compassion and respect. You should be able to detect the staff's caring attitude toward the residents.

20. Were residents walking or moving independently about the facility with or without assistive devices such as canes, walkers, or wheelchairs?
    Generally, you should see some residents up and moving about the facility. It is important to encourage older adults to be as active as possible. Maintaining or regaining mobility is a primary goal for most residents.

21. Was there a feeling of life and activity about the facility?
    The facility should feel like a place where people live. It is the residents' home and should appear as a home, not a hotel. Residents should be comfortably engaged in activities.

22. How often is a nurse (RN or LPN) present in the facility? (May need to ask staff.)
    There should be enough staff on duty so that you see them working about the facility as you tour. It is important that staff be present to assist residents with scheduled and unscheduled needs.

23. Did residents have a variety of foods to choose from at mealtime? (Look for posted meal plans; may need to ask staff.)

24. Did residents have access to snacks and other foods at any time? (Look for posted signs about access to snacks; may need to ask staff.)
    Having choices in foods for meals and snacks promotes good nutrition and satisfaction with food services. Food and drink should be available between meals.

25. Were a variety of activities available for residents? (Look for posted schedules, calendars, group meetings, etc.)

    Activities should appeal to a variety of people. Although some residents will continue to pursue activities they enjoyed before coming to the assisted-living facility, there should be a variety of daily activities so that residents can socialize, explore new interests, and occupy their time.

26. Were there activities involving children? (Look for posted activities schedules, calendars.)

27. Did residents have access to telephone communication? (May need to ask staff.)

    Maintaining contact with friends and family is important to residents' emotional well-being. Residents should have access to a phone where they can call friends and family. Is the phone in a private area where they can have a private conversation? Are there phone jacks in resident rooms, which would allow phones to be installed?

28. Did residents have access to e-mail or other computer-based communication? (May need to ask staff.)

    Ask whether the facility has an Internet connection that allows residents to e-mail friends or family. Can residents access the computer without staff being present? Are residents encouraged or allowed to have computers in their apartments?

29. Were the hallways well lighted?

30. Were the common areas well lighted?
    As we age, our eyesight declines. For residents' safety, comfort, and ability to move about the facility, it is important that they be able to see well. Lighting should be adequate for all activities with minimal glare. Natural light in all areas is important.

31. Were there pets (dogs, cats, birds, etc.) and/or live plants in the facility?
    Since this is home to residents, they should be allowed and encouraged to have plants or other things in their rooms that make it homelike. Plants should be placed throughout the facility. Many consider the presence of pets—in residents' rooms and in non-food service areas—to be indicators of good quality.

32. Were the pets and/or plants in good condition?
    Any plants or pets in the facility should be in good condition. The staff is responsible for the facility's appearance and for pet care, including helping residents care for their pets.

33. Were there outdoor gardens or other outdoor spaces for residents to enjoy?

34. Did residents have access to outdoor spaces?
    Some residents prefer to spend many hours outdoors and should be able to do so if they wish. The outdoor space should be safe, large enough to accommodate residents, clean, and well maintained. Shaded and wind-sheltered areas should be available.

Interviewing staff in an assisted-living facility

If you have visited an assisted-living facility and found that it has good care, ask to interview the staff member who handles admissions. In most small facilities, that person is the administrator or manager. You may have to make an appointment for this interview.

Below you'll find a list of detailed interview questions about costs, payment options, staff workload, continuity of management and staff, safety information, and more. Each question includes the answer you're likely to hear if the facility is doing a good job.

The actual questionnaire (without the answers below), which begins on page 83, includes space for taking notes. Copy this questionnaire and take it with you to interviews. Note that many of the issues covered here—such as helping residents transition to life in assisted living—are covered in greater detail in chapters 5 and 6.

Cost

- Does this facility accept some sort of public assistance or is private pay the only form of payment?

  Mostly, people pay their own costs for assisted living. Some states offer Medicaid funds to help out seniors. Learn about what payment options are available in each facility and whether Medicaid funds are available to help with expenses. If you have long-term care insurance, check whether it pays for assisted living. Plans vary. If you need help, check with your plan's company. Ask if any residents have used long-term care insurance to pay for expenses at the facility.

- What are the basic weekly and monthly charges?

  Charges begin at about $80 to $100 per day and can go much higher, depending on the services included, the size of the room or apartment, and location.

- What items are not covered in the basic charge?

  Medication costs are not included in assisted-living charges, so be sure to ask about how medications are purchased and what the typical costs will be. Facilities often have additional charges for things like:

wheelchairs	*dietary supplements*
transportation	*incontinence supplies*
dental care	*podiatry care*
beauty/barber shop	*physical, occupational, or speech therapy*

- Will staff notify residents before supplying any service not covered by insurance?

  Facilities should notify residents before rendering services for which they charge extra. If a resident designates another person to handle billing, then the facility should notify that person in advance.

- Is an advance payment, or deposit, required? If so, will residents get the money back when they leave the facility?

  Some facilities require one or two months' payment in advance. They should return all or part of this if the resident leaves.

Building and rooms

- Can residents bring furniture from home?

  Residents should be allowed—and encouraged—to bring chairs, a dresser, or other pieces of furniture, as well as pictures and other personal items that make a room or apartment more homelike.

- Can residents bring a pet?

  Some facilities encourage residents to bring a family pet, generally as long as the pet is sociable and the resident is able to tend to it. At some places, the staff helps out with pet care.

- Can pets visit?

  Pet visitation should be encouraged. Be sure the pet is clean, and be mindful of proper disposal of animal waste. Also remember that other residents or family members may not enjoy animals.

- Is there adequate storage space for personal items, both in the room and in a general storage area?

  Each resident's room or apartment should have space to store personal items used frequently, plus space for a few items of off-season clothing, small seasonal decorations, and other items. Family members may want to store residents' belongings at home, especially valuable items.

- If this is a multistory building, are there adequate elevators to transport residents?

  There should be enough elevators for residents to easily get from place to place. Be sure to see for yourself that the elevators are adequate.

- Is there outdoor space for residents to enjoy?

  Residents should be able to spend time outdoors. Since some people may wander, facilities should offer a safe outdoor space that prevents them from leaving the grounds.

- How are smokers' and nonsmokers' wishes addressed? (If smoking is allowed, how are smokers' and nonsmokers' wishes addressed?)

  Many facilities have smoke-free buildings and grounds for all residents, staff, and visitors. Be sure to ask. If smoking for residents is allowed, residents should have a separate, well-ventilated area where they may safely smoke without polluting the air for others. Staff smoking areas (if allowed) should not be at a public entrance.

- How does the staff know if residents leave the building?

  In cases where residents should not leave the building without supervision, doors should have alarms to alert staff when residents leave. Some facilities use electronic devices that sound an alarm when residents pass through the doorway.

- In case of fire, does the building have a sprinkler system?

  It should have sprinklers.

- If there is a fire, how will the staff make sure the residents are safe?

  The staff should have a detailed plan and be able to explain it.

Staff

- How long have the last two administrator/managers worked here?

  It's best when administrators stay for five or more years. A facility with a stable administration is more likely to deliver better services than one with constant turnover.

- How long have the last two nurse managers/consultants worked here?

  A director of nursing who stays for five or more years is likely to have staff and care delivery systems in place. Turnover in this position could indicate problems in delivery of care.

- How long has the current owner of the facility owned and operated it?

  Facilities with stable, long-term ownership are more likely to have the staff and care delivery systems in place than those that change ownership frequently.

- Is a licensed nurse available every day?

  Although no federal regulations set staffing levels for licensed nurses (RNs or LPNs) in assisted living, a licensed nurse should be on-site daily. Licensed practical nurses (LPNs) have about a year of education and training beyond high school. Their job is to evaluate residents' needs and see that each resident gets the care that he or she requires.

- Is a registered nurse (RN) available to the residents at least weekly or more often?

  Registered nurses have two to four years of college education. They are responsible for knowing each resident's medical conditions and recognizing when there are changes that need attention. If they see each resident at least weekly, they will get to know them well enough to notice significant physical or emotional changes.

- How many nursing assistants work during each shift?

  Nursing assistants provide most of the personal care, such as helping residents eat, dress, bathe, and go to the toilet. There should be plenty of assistants to help all the residents. Federal regulations do not mandate specific numbers of nursing assistant staff members, so availability will vary depending on recruitment, staffing policies at the facility, and the kind of care that residents need.

- Are the nursing assistants certified?

  Certified nursing assistants take a state-approved nursing assistant course with both classroom and practical experience with residents. Personal care assistants are trained by the facility. It is important that personal care staff are trained to care for older people and recognize problems that may occur. Be sure to ask about how much training nursing assistants have had and how much continuing education all staff members in the facility have routinely to keep them up-to-date.

- Do residents have the same nursing assistants or personal care assistant helping them day in and day out?

  That's the best situation. When staff members work with the same residents, they can get to know them, and this often improves the quality of care.

- Do residents have the same housekeeper cleaning their room each time?

  It's reassuring to residents when they get to know the housecleaning staff members, who often become a source of social support.

- Does this facility use staff from a temporary employment agency?

  Temporary workers can't know the residents and their special needs, so using them consistently can cause problems. Occasional backup from an agency may be necessary, especially in some urban areas where businesses must compete for quality staff members. However, it's a red flag if a facility routinely relies on temporary workers.

- Does this facility do criminal background checks on all employees?

  All healthcare facilities should do criminal background checks. It is important that older adults not be cared for by people with criminal histories.

- How much are nursing assistants, housekeepers, and dietary staff paid? How does this compare to wages paid by other assisted-living facilities in the community?

  Wages should be comparable to those at other facilities or to what other healthcare providers make in the community. Workers who are fairly compensated are more likely to stay with their employers, and this often results in a higher quality of care. As you visit different facilities, you'll get a better idea of how their wages compare.

- Is a registered dietitian available?

  A registered dietitian should be available to consult with the dietary staff and review meal plans.

- Are physical therapy, speech therapy, and occupational therapy available?

  Rehabilitation therapists are usually available from home-health agencies and can provide periodic rehabilitation services to assisted-living residents. Ask staff if they have successfully used therapy services from a particular agency or another source, and inquire about the costs of these services.

- Do primary care providers make visits to see residents in the facility, or do residents make clinic appointments for seeing their healthcare provider?

  Typically, when residents living in assisted living need to see a physician or other healthcare provider, the resident will need transportation to the provider's clinic. This is unlike the nursing home setting, where physicians and other healthcare providers come to the nursing home to see residents.

Transition to facility life

- How does the staff help new residents adjust to the facility?

  Staff members should be able to explain how they help new residents adjust. They might use a welcome banner, staff visits, events such as new residents' teas, and other efforts to involve new residents in social and exercise activities.

- How do current residents help new residents adjust to the facility?

  They may hold a resident visitation, form a welcome committee, or come up with other ways to greet new residents and help them become part of the community.

- What are typical problems that new residents have when they come to this facility? How does the staff help them handle these problems?

  The staff should be able to explain common problems that concern new residents and how they can help.

- How are residents matched as roommates? (Not applicable for facilities with only private rooms.)

The staff should try to match interests, healthcare needs, ability to get along, and other characteristics. Some facilities have two beds per room, though most also offer private rooms or apartments.

- What happens if roommates do not get along? (Not applicable for facilities with only private rooms.)

  Residents should have some recourse if they cannot get along with their roommate. The staff may suggest another roommate, or they might arrange a meeting between the roommates and help them resolve conflicts.

- Do residents refer to the assisted-living facility as "my home now"?

  Ideally, as residents adjust, they tend to refer to the facility as their home.

- Are there other residents here who might be interested in socializing?

  Staff should be aware of other residents who may be a good social match.

Opportunities for resident and family input

- Is there a family advisory or support group?

  There should be. Family groups can help residents and their families adjust to assisted living.

- Do families and residents meet routinely with the administrator/manager, nurses, or the other staff to discuss care and life issues?

  All concerned parties should be able to meet with the staff to discuss care concerns and share ideas to make life in assisted living even better.

- Is there a resident council?

  Many facilities have a resident council where residents routinely meet with the staff to discuss issues that are important to residents, such as services, care, and meals.

- Is there a family council?

  Many homes have family councils where families can routinely advise the staff about care and quality-of-life issues to improve service.

Care issues

- What do residents usually say about the food?

  The staff should know if residents generally like the food or if they prefer certain menu offerings to others.

- What happens if a resident does not want to eat a particular meal?

  Residents should have alternatives. Ask what substitutions are available to residents.

- Are residents able to request special food items?

  Residents should be able to make special requests, and families should be encouraged to bring in special foods that their family member likes.

- May I taste the food and observe a meal?

  The staff should let you taste a meal prepared for the residents. Watch workers serve a meal. The food should look and smell appetizing. The ambiance in the dining room should be pleasant and appealing.

- Is there a program to help residents regain their physical abilities?

Most facilities offer exercise or walking programs as part of the basic daily care rate, but you should ask to confirm. If there is a separate charge, ask what residents gain from the program and how much it costs.

- Are residents assisted to the bathroom when they ask?

  They should be.

- Are toilets conveniently located for residents?

  They should be.

- Are there grab bars and other safety devices in residents' bathrooms?

  There should be.

- Is bathing assistance available if needed?

  It should be. Also, look at bathing areas. They should be private, warm, and inviting to use.

- Is there an emergency call system?

  Although assisted-living facilities do not typically have call lights, which are standard in nursing homes and hospitals, they should have emergency call systems in each bathroom and bedroom. Staff should be able to explain how they respond to emergency calls.

- What activities are available?

  There should be a variety of activities to interest a variety of people. Many facilities offer craft groups; music groups; shopping trips; exercise groups; small discussion groups; games like bingo and bunko; and field trips to fairs, festivals, and other community events. In addition, staff members should encourage individual activities, such as reading and playing cards. There should also be activities for residents with reduced mental capacities.

- How frequently are activities offered?

  Activities should occur often so that residents can socialize, explore new interests, and occupy their time. Occasional evening and weekend activities should supplement traditional midmorning and midafternoon events.

- Do residents go to religious services in the community? Is transportation available? Are religious services or activities available in the facility?

  Residents should have access to community religious services. Typically, transportation is available to local places of worship. Groups commonly engage in Bible study or other religious activities. Ask about services or other religious activities that will meet your needs.

- Do residents have frequent outings for shopping or other leisure activities?

  Outings should be frequent and include trips to shopping areas, recreational areas, community events, and other nearby locations. Staff should encourage families to take loved ones out to favorite restaurants, family celebrations, or other events of interest.

- How does the staff help residents who are depressed?

  Staff members should be able to describe a number of techniques, including talking frequently with the residents, trying to involve them in activities, and getting a psychological evaluation for the resident.

- Who is the ombudsman for this facility? Does the ombudsman visit regularly?

All assisted-living facilities, board-and-care facilities, and nursing homes have a consumer advocate who is a part of the official state ombudsman program. Ombudsmen investigate and attempt to resolve concerns raised by residents, and their families and friends. The staff should be able to tell you who the ombudsman is and when he or she usually comes to the facility to see residents. To locate the ombudsman in your area, visit www.ltcombudsman.org/static_pages/ombudsmen.cfm.

Special Alzheimer's assisted-living facilities

Some assisted-living facilities specialize in caring for people with Alzheimer's disease or other kinds of dementia. These facilities are designed for people with Alzheimer's disease and can help them stay independent and active in a safe, secure, and homelike environment. Often the facility is small, serving twelve to fifteen residents. Each resident has a private room for sleeping and shares common spaces, much like in a large home. Some facilities involve residents in preparing food, taking part in activities in a large living room, or performing normal everyday activities like doing laundry and setting tables for meals. Such places have outdoor spaces where residents can walk out of doors, but where they cannot wander away from the facility or into traffic.

Like residents of other assisted-living facilities, residents in Alzheimer's facilities typically pay for everything themselves. Be sure to ask about costs and whether the state provides funds for people who need financial assistance. Also ask the following questions about the care and staff training in special Alzheimer's assisted living.

- How are the services and activities in this facility designed for residents with Alzheimer's disease?

  Because residents with Alzheimer's or other dementias have special needs, facilities should offer certain services. For example, a quiet environment can minimize confusion and reduce agitated behavior. Special activities can help occupy residents and minimize wandering. Involving residents in normal daily activities like setting the table, folding laundry, helping with gardening, helping with preparing meals, etc., helps residents engage in living and enjoy each day.

- Is the staff specially trained to care for people with Alzheimer's disease?

  They should be.

- Are doors secured or fitted with alarms so that residents with Alzheimer's cannot wander outside without a staff member?

  All doors leading out of the building or into areas that contain supplies or equipment should be secure. Many Alzheimer's facilities are designed so that residents have limited indoor and outdoor spaces where they can safely wander. In some facilities, residents can go outside into safe areas alone when they want, but staff can see them at all times. In this case, the doors to these safe areas do not need alarms.

- Do residents have a safe space to enjoy the outdoors? Is it designed so that they can enjoy it frequently or when they choose to do so?

  Many residents with Alzheimer's disease or other dementias enjoy outdoor spaces. Facilities should offer inviting outdoor spaces that provide shade in warm weather and shelter from wind in colder weather. Residents must not be able to wander away from the building or into areas where they might be harmed.

Questions for staff at assisted-living facilities

Facility ______________________ Date __________ Time __________

Cost

1. Does this facility accept some sort of public assistance or is private pay the only form of payment?

2. What are the basic weekly and monthly charges?

3. What items are not covered in the basic charges?
   - ❒ Medications
   - ❒ Dietary supplements
   - ❒ Beauty/barber shop
   - ❒ Incontinence supplies
   - ❒ Wheelchair
   - ❒ Transportation
   - ❒ Dentist
   - ❒ Podiatry care
   - ❒ Physical, occupational, or speech therapy

4. Before residents receive any service not covered by insurance, such as dental care, will staff notify them or their financial designee?

5. Is an advanced payment, or deposit, required? If so, will it be returned if the resident leaves the facility?

Building and rooms

6. Can residents bring furniture from home?

7. Can residents bring a pet?

8. Can pets visit?

9. Is there adequate storage space for personal items, both in the room and in a general storage area?

10. If this is a multistory building, are there adequate elevators to transport residents?

11. Is there outdoor space for residents to enjoy?

12. How are smokers' and nonsmokers' wishes addressed?

13. How does the staff know if residents leave the building?

14. In case of fire, does the building have a sprinkler system?

15. If there is a fire, how will the staff make sure the residents are safe?

Staff

16. How long have the last two administrator/managers worked here?

17. How long have the last two nurse managers/consultants worked here?

18. How long has the current owner of the facility owned and operated it?

19. Is a licensed nurse available every day?

20. Is a registered nurse (RN) available to the residents at least weekly or more often?

21. How many nursing assistants work during each shift?

22. Are the nursing assistants certified?

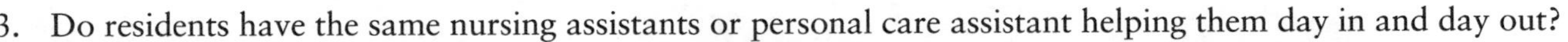

23. Do residents have the same nursing assistants or personal care assistant helping them day in and day out?

24. Do residents have the same housekeeper cleaning their room each time?

25. Does this facility use staff from a temporary employment agency?

26. Does this facility do criminal background checks on all employees?

27. How much are nursing assistants, housekeepers, and dietary staff paid? How does this compare to wages paid by other assisted-living facilities in the community?

28. Is a registered dietitian available?

29. Are physical therapy, speech therapy, and occupational therapy available?

30. Do primary care providers make visits to see residents in the facility, or do residents make clinic appointments for seeing their healthcare provider?

Transition to facility life

31. How does the staff help new residents adjust to the facility?

32. How do current residents help new residents adjust to the facility?

33. What are typical problems that new residents have when they come to this facility? How does the staff help them handle these problems?

34. How are residents matched as roommates? (Does not apply to facilities with only private rooms.)

35. What happens if roommates do not get along? (Does not apply to facilities with only private rooms.)

36. Do residents refer to the assisted-living facility as "my home now"?

37. Are there other residents here who might be interested in socializing?

Opportunities for input from residents and families

38. Is there a family advisory or support group?

39. Do families and residents meet routinely with the administrator/manager, nurses, or the other staff to discuss care and life issues?

40. Is there a resident council?

41. Is there a family council?

Care issues

42. What do residents usually say about the food?

43. What happens if a resident does not want to eat a particular meal?

44. Are residents able to request special food items?

45. May I taste the food and observe a meal?

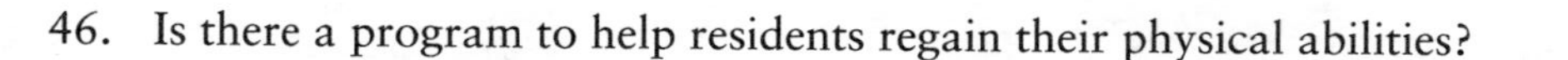

46. Is there a program to help residents regain their physical abilities?

47. Are residents assisted to the bathroom when they ask?

48. Are toilets conveniently located for residents?

49. Are there grab bars and other safety devices in residents' bathrooms?

50. Is bathing assistance available if needed?

51. Is there an emergency call system?

52. What activities are available?

53. How frequently are activities offered?

54. Do residents go to religious services in the community? Is transportation available? Do religious services or activities take place in the facility?

55. Do residents have frequent outings for shopping or other leisure activities?

56. How does the staff help residents who are depressed?

57. Who is the ombudsman for this facility? Does the ombudsman visit regularly?

Alzheimer's care

58. How are the services and activities in this facility designed for residents with Alzheimer's disease?

59. Is the staff specially trained to care for people with Alzheimer's disease?

60. Are doors secured or fitted with alarms so that residents with Alzheimer's cannot wander outside without a staff member?

61. Do residents have a safe space to enjoy the outdoors? Is it designed so that they can enjoy it frequently or when they choose to do so?

Interviewing families of residents in an assisted-living facility

When you think you've found an assisted-living facility that's a good fit, we recommend interviewing family members of some residents. Strike up conversations with other visitors as you tour the facility. Tell them what you are considering, and ask if they'd be willing to talk about their experiences.

This chapter contains key questions to help you glean others' impressions of a facility's staff and policies. As elsewhere, we provide a sample of a "good" answer for each question.

The actual questionnaire (without the answers below) is on pages 98–101. Make as many copies as you need, and use a new copy for each interview. Feel free to ask your own questions as well.

- Does your loved one seem to enjoy certain parts of the day (events, mealtimes, etc.), every day?

  The resident should. Ask family members for examples.

- Do staff members treat your loved one with respect and courtesy?

  They should. Ask for examples.

- Are residents encouraged to be as independent as possible?

  They should strive for independence, though abilities differ among residents.

- How often do you visit?

  Responses will vary. Try to get a sense of whether people feel they must visit to make sure the staff is taking care of their loved one. Also, try to learn whether they're afraid to leave their family member alone for some reason.

- Is the staff positive toward your visits?

  They should be. If not, ask the family why.

- Is there an emergency call system that your loved one can use? Are staff members responsive to the emergency calls and other requests for care?

  In assisted living, residents should use such calls only in true emergencies. A staff member should arrive within minutes. To help keep emergencies to a minimum, staff should be responsive to other requests and care needs and see that needs are met in a timely fashion.

- Do the same staff members regularly help your loved one?

  The more they do, the better the care is likely to be.

- Do staff members seem to know your loved one as a person? Are they able to talk to your loved one about details of his or her life?

  The staff should know the residents well, and they should be receptive to residents who share details of their lives.

- Does the staff know what kind of care your loved one needs?

  They should.

- Do you think the staff takes proper care of your loved one?

  Although few family members are experts in care for older people, observation and intuition should tell them whether their loved one is well cared for.

- Has your loved one ever complained of not being treated well?

  If so, ask them to tell you the story. Did staff members seem to be deliberately mistreating the resident?

- Do you think the staff listens to you?

  Families should feel that staff members listen, and they should be able to give you an example or two to support this perception.

- Does your loved one feel like this is home now?

  That is ideal, but remember that it can take time. Find out how long this person has been a resident. Generally, most residents adjust to the move in a few weeks or months.

- Are residents and families involved in the life of the assisted-living facility?

  Staff should ask family members to be involved in residents' lives and take part in the facility's activities. Staff should schedule appropriate events that help involve residents and engage families and others in the community. Find out how others are involved in the life of the facility.

- Does the staff follow up on requests by residents or families?

  Family members should be able to offer an example or two of how the staff followed through on such issues.

- Is your loved one fearful of complaining?

  Residents should be able to state reasonable complaints without fear. Fearfulness is common among people who feel vulnerable, so staff should help residents feel safe and able to voice complaints.

- If you complain, how does the staff deal with your complaints?

  Try to get a sense of the family member's complaint, how they broached it, and how the staff responded.

- Have you been concerned about personal items being lost or misplaced?

  This may happen occasionally. It should not be common. Personal items can be difficult to keep track of, so mark them clearly to help staff members put them back where they belong. Store valuable items, such as heirloom jewelry, at home. Provide costume jewelry for a loved one to wear. If it is misplaced, you will not have lost a family keepsake.

- If your loved one is injured or becomes ill, does the staff contact you quickly?

  They should.

- Does your loved one feel safe and secure in this facility?

  He or she should.

- Have you ever been concerned about your loved one's safety?

  Although assisted-living facilities are not risk-free, listen for excessive concern. Ask what the family knows about security precautions at the facility and their effectiveness.

- Knowing what you know now, if you had to choose an assisted-living facility today, would you still select this one?

  If the family is satisfied with the care and services, they would.

Questions for family members of residents in an assisted-living facility

Facility ______________ Name ______________ Date ________ Time ________

1. Does your loved one seem to enjoy certain parts of the day (events, mealtimes, etc.), every day?

2. Do staff members treat your loved one with respect and courtesy?

3. Are residents encouraged to be as independent as possible?

4. How often do you visit?

5. Is the staff positive toward your visits?

6. Is there an emergency call system that your loved one can use? Are staff members responsive to the emergency calls and other requests for care?

7. Do the same staff members regularly help your loved one?

8. Do staff members seem to know your loved one as a person? Are they able to talk to your loved one about details of his or her life?

9. Does the staff know what kind of care your loved one needs?

10. Do you think the staff takes proper care of your loved one?

11. Has your loved one ever complained of not being treated well?

12. Do you think the staff listens to you?

13. Does your loved one feel like this is home now?

14. Are residents and families involved in the life of the assisted-living facility?

15. Does the staff follow up on requests by residents or families?

16. Is your loved one fearful of complaining?

17. If you complain, how does the staff deal with your complaints?

18. Have you been concerned about personal items being lost or misplaced?

19. If your loved one is injured or becomes ill, does the staff contact you quickly?

20. Does your loved one feel safe and secure in this facility?

21. Have you ever been concerned about your loved one's safety?

22. Knowing what you know now, if you had to choose an assisted-living facility today, would you still select this one?

CHAPTER FIVE

Nursing Homes: Making a Decision about Quality of Care

If you bring up the topic of nursing homes with most people, you're likely to get a negative response. Plenty of undesirable images pop to mind—lack of privacy, bad smells, poor food, inadequate staff, separation from friends and family, an unpleasant environment. But this doesn't have to be the case. More and more, nursing homes are defying such stereotypes. These "improved" nursing homes are moving away from the institutional, hospital-like settings of the past to offer more homelike, personalized care. In these improved nursing homes, staff members are more visible and attentive, family members are more involved, and facilities are cleaner and friendlier.

When we say "improved nursing homes," we're not talking about newly constructed or recently remodeled facilities. Instead, we're talking about new attitudes toward what nursing homes and other long-term care facilities can and should be. The age of the physical building is less important than the number of staff who work on-site, the range of activities available, the quality of personal care and healthcare, and the overall pleasantness of the environment. To put it another way, the "improved nursing homes" are those progressive long-term care facilities that offer the highest-quality care for their residents.

What are the signs of quality care?

Our research on nursing homes has led us to identify seven key aspects of quality care, which we label homelike surroundings, care delivery, grooming, communication, basic environment, odor, and access to environments. These features have been distilled from our research on nursing homes, but as we've seen in earlier chapters, they also apply to other long-term care settings. And because many people will eventually need the services of a nursing home, if only for a short-term recuperative stay, the information that follows should prove useful no matter what long-term care option you choose.

Homelike surroundings

As its name implies, a nursing home should feel like a home, not like an institution or hospital. It should have the look and feel of an active place where people live and where they receive the care they need. It should be buzzing with life, hope, activity, and caring individuals. Each room should have plants and personal items so that each resident can regard the room as his or her own. Local community groups should visit residents. A volunteer program should be active, involving children and pets and promoting a variety of group activities.

The mission of the nursing home should be obvious to all who live, work, and visit there. The top priority should be caring for residents and their families. Yes, nursing homes are businesses, and they need to watch the bottom line, but consumers say loud and clear that nursing homes should, first and foremost, take care of residents. A most welcome refrain for all to hear is when residents say, "This is home now."

Care delivery and grooming

A high-quality nursing home is one where the staff stays on top of the fundamentals of care, including:

- Help with bathing, eating, and going to the bathroom;
- Keeping residents' hair, teeth, and clothes clean;
- Offering a variety of good food to eat in a sociable setting;
- Helping people stay involved socially;
- Arranging for medical help when necessary; and
- Minimizing the occurrence of injuries and property loss. (These happen at one's own home, too, don't forget.)

A key reason that people move into nursing homes is to have professional staff monitor conditions that may have become too complex or unstable for them or their family members to manage at home. It may be that their chronic illnesses need continuous assessment and managing by RNs, or their care directed for more comfort as people approach the end of life. Sometimes managing end-of-life care is best managed where there is staff twenty-four hours each day, RNs to help with pain management, and nursing assistants to help with personal care needs.

Another key reason that people move into nursing homes is for rehabilitation. When older people are hospitalized with serious illnesses, they may need to spend some rehabilitation time in a nursing home. Rehabilitation helps them regain functional abilities like walking, caring for themselves, and gaining strength to once again manage at home. Many nursing home residents receive rehabilitation so that they can again live at home on their own.

Residents, families, and staff members should work together so residents get the special attention they want and need. One resident explained, "I want to know that the nurses are doing my care the way it should be done for *me*, not just for anybody. I have certain conditions and I know they need to be managed in certain ways so I don't get sick." Nursing home workers also should get to know each resident's history. One daughter remarked that "the staff should know that my dad was a farmer all his life and is likely to wake up very early because he milked cows for many years."

Residents need to be engaged in activities for their enjoyment and benefit. Staff members in "improved nursing homes" make these activities fun and work to involve even reluctant residents. Look for variety: games, music groups, religious study groups, physical fitness programs, and current events discussions. Staff members encourage residents to get involved in activities and are responsive and compassionate with residents. Staff members as well as residents are clean and well groomed. A well-trained, well-paid staff will generally stick around, and residents benefit from that continuity.

Nursing homes should be well staffed, with the same staff members caring for the same residents each day. Registered nurses must be closely involved in resident care to evaluate medical conditions and be alert to changes that need attention. Nurses who specialize in geriatric care should supervise, ensuring that residents get the care they need.

Communication

Family members often mention that communication—between staff and families, staff and residents, among staff members—is a crucial component of quality care. It's important that staff members hear—perhaps more than once—about each resident's needs, likes, dislikes, and habits. There should be positive verbal and nonverbal communication between staff and residents. Staff and residents should greet each other and feel comfortable with each other. Good staff members will talk with residents and listen to what they have to say. You should see staff and residents smiling and perhaps joking with each other. Above all, you should have the sense that residents are treated with dignity and respect.

Basic environment

Consumers, families, and staff members all agree that a nursing home should be clean and odor free. It should be spacious and not too noisy. It should feel like a pleasant place to live. The grounds around the facility should be inviting and accessible to residents, families, and community groups. The building should be well lighted, with lots of windows so that residents can see outdoors. Furnishings and equipment should be functional and well maintained. This means that beds are low enough to minimize falls; tables are the right height for eating comfortably; and chairs are sturdy, with arms to help people stand up easily and safely. Floors should be nonslip and without glare. In general, the environment should be safe and free from obvious hazards.

Odor

Odor is a key indicator of quality. If you enter a nursing home and are overpowered by the odor of urine, feces, or perspiration, just turn around and walk out. Even if you have made an appointment, leave. This is not a place where you or your loved one would want to live. But don't despair—good nursing homes are out there. Keep looking.

Access to environments

It is important that residents can use common spaces that are enjoyable, functional, and homelike. Even residents with cognitive impairments like Alzheimer's disease or other dementias need to have access to common spaces, particularly outdoor garden areas. The nursing home should design ways for residents to enjoy being outdoors and at the same time be safe from wandering into potentially dangerous places if wandering is a problem.

Families and other visitors also need access to pleasant places to enjoy visiting with loved ones. It is important to have some private space to talk, as well as larger spaces to enjoy with other residents, visitors, and staff. Many improved nursing homes have a kitchen space for residents and families so they can enjoy a cup of coffee or snack together, or perhaps enjoy cooking a pizza or cookies for a treat while visiting.

Families need to be involved

Improved nursing homes encourage families to get involved with their loved ones' care. And family members say that spending time at the nursing home ensures that residents are fed, exercised, and medicated properly and in a timely fashion. When families work closely with staff members and really get to know them, they feel more confident that their loved ones are receiving the sort of personalized care they want them to have.

Getting involved often means hands-on work, such as washing clothes, bringing in favorite foods, or leading group activities. Some family members get so involved that they become political advocates for nursing home reform. Nursing homes are highly regulated by government agencies, and family members have testified before state and federal bodies about such issues as the need for increased recruitment, training, and reimbursement of nursing home staff. Highly involved volunteers may even join the board that operates the nursing home or advises the home's administrator about care issues.

Frequently, family members form advisory or support groups. Because families often have similar concerns, they can be a great source of strength and support for each other. Families might also form networks to watch out for each other's relatives, something like a "neighborhood watch."

Consumers and nursing home workers often have differing perspectives on the meaning of quality. To achieve true quality care, both customers and staff members need to imagine themselves in the others' position.

From the consumer's point of view, a good staff is paramount. As one family member said, "Without staff, nothing else is possible." Consumers have suggested that nursing assistants, who are the main providers of direct care to residents, should participate in orientation programs in which they spend a day or more as residents. Consumers want staff members to know how it feels to be given a shower in a shower chair, to be fed a meal, or to have to wait to be taken to the bathroom.

On the other hand, staff members see themselves working as hard as they can to do as much as they can for many people with different needs. They sometimes forget that residents see them as the center of their universe. It may serve you well to let staff members know how important they are to your family. Sometimes, too, staff members are unaware of how beneficial family involvement can be. Families may need to take the initiative to get more directly involved in their loved ones' care.

How do I evaluate the quality of a nursing home?

One way to evaluate the quality of a nursing home is to examine its inspection history. Nursing homes are subject to close federal and state inspections, which are a matter of public record. Request the most recent state survey from any facility you are considering or find the survey inspection report by going to www.medicare.gov and clicking on the link to compare nursing homes. But remember, the survey may be a year old—conditions may have changed considerably for the better or worse. Your observations about quality of care are very important in making a good decision.

The government inspections, which occur at least every fifteen months, are meant to ensure that facilities meet minimum federal and state requirements regarding the building, sanitation, basic care and services, staffing, and administration. Although homes should have few violations, even a spotless inspection record does not guarantee a high-quality nursing home. Good-quality care goes beyond the regulations. The inspection record is just one piece of information you will need to make an informed decision about long-term care.

Another document that might help you evaluate nursing home quality is a facility's "quality measures" report (available for all Medicare- and Medicaid-certified nursing homes). This is a tabulation of the problems experienced by the residents at that particular nursing home. Quality measures quantify such problems as need for help with daily activities; residents who spend most of their time in bed or in a chair; or residents with pain, pressure sores, physical restraints, depression or anxiety, loose control of bowel or bladder, bladder catheters, urinary tract infections, or excessive weight loss. Scores for each nursing home are compared with those of other facilities in the state.

There is also a quality ratings score from a low of one star to a high of five stars. These scores are based on survey results, staffing, and quality measures. Before visiting a home, you can access the home's quality measures and rating score report by going to www.medicare.gov and clicking on the link to compare nursing homes.

Other sources to help assess nursing home quality are listed in chapter 7. We provide numerous Web sites that can help you locate government reports, government contact information, and consumer advocacy groups. We also list the ombudsman programs for each state. An ombudsman is a consumer advocate who helps investigate and resolve complaints made by nursing home residents, their families, or their friends. Perhaps the easiest way to locate your ombudsman is to call a local nursing home. The staff will know the ombudsman and how to contact him or her. Or, you can locate the area's ombudsman by visiting www.ltcombudsman.org/static_pages/help.cfm.

Other helpful Web sites about nursing homes include:

- www.helpguide.org/elder/nursing_homes_skilled_nursing_facilities.htm
- nursinghomeaction.org
- www.aarp.org/bulletin/
- www.advisor.com/boomer/story/plan-effective-senior-facility-care-plan-meeting

Although information from government reports, consumer groups, and your ombudsman can be useful, the only way you can be sure you've found a good-quality nursing home is to inspect it yourself. Government reports will only tell you whether a nursing home meets minimum standards. Ombudsmen and consumer groups will only tell you if a nursing home has a history of problems or complaints. To learn about the positive aspects of a nursing home—to discover whether that home demonstrates the key signs of quality care—you must visit the facility yourself. And to make this visit as effective and efficient as possible, you need a guide that clearly defines what you should look for, how you should rate what you see, what questions you should ask, and what answers you should receive. Such a guide is provided for you on pages 125–131. We also provide evaluation forms that you can photocopy and take along when touring different facilities. Using this book, you will be able to walk through any nursing home and rate its quality of care in a half hour or less.

The walk-through

Now that we know the seven signs of quality—homelike surroundings, care delivery, grooming, communication, basic environment, odor, and access to environments—the next step is to visit and compare facilities. Shop around. Selecting a nursing home may be one of the most difficult choices you'll have to make. You can expect to visit several nursing homes before making your decision. As you look, always remember that you are searching for the best possible quality care.

Start by looking at the nursing homes in your community—you may find that the best one is close to home. Convenience is great, but if you are not satisfied with local facilities, keep looking. It is better to find a good facility farther from your home than settle for substandard care close by. We have talked to many families who agree.

When considering a facility, call and make an appointment to take a tour. Or, just go to the facility to make your own observations and talk with some of the staff. When you are ready, explain to a staff member that you are looking for a nursing home and ask if you can take a tour.

Taking a tour is your best opportunity to evaluate a facility, so make the most of it as you walk through. On pages 116–123, you will find a detailed questionnaire to guide you. It tells you specifically what to watch for and how to judge quality of care. Make as many copies of this questionnaire as you need, and take a copy along on every tour. Then, after visiting several facilities, you can look back on your notes and compare them.

We based the walk-through questions on years of research with consumers and providers of nursing home care. The questionnaire has been tested in hundreds of nursing homes, so we're confident that it will help you in your search.

Before answering the walk-through questions, we recommend that you tour the facility for a few minutes during general business hours (between 10 a.m. and 6 p.m.). Walk through common living spaces, hallways, and other public areas. Ask yourself, "Is this a place where I would feel comfortable living?" Be a good observer; think about what you see, hear, smell, and feel. Listen to your senses and trust your judgment.

A note about choosing your answers: The multiple-choice answers range from 1 to 5, with 1 being the worst quality of care and 5 indicating the best. Be sure to answer every question that applies to that facility. If you have difficulty scoring a particular question, you may need to walk though some areas a second time. To answer certain questions, you may to ask staff about the care and services (questions 7, 8, 22, 23, 24, and 25).

For best results, add up the scores for the questions for a total score. This "quality score" will range from 30 to 150. A score of 30 indicates the lowest quality of care; 150 indicates the highest. Our research shows that scores of 128 or higher suggest a good-quality nursing home. Homes scoring 103 or lower suggest a nursing home that has quality problems, so keep looking. Scores between 116 and 150 are typical of most facilities. The higher the score, the more likely you are to be satisfied with the care and services, so make sure you have found the best facility in your area. Driving a bit farther for good care is worth it in the long run.

We know from our research that the questionnaire works best if you take the tour with a friend or family member who also scores the facility. Don't talk to each other about your answers until you have both answered all questions. Then talk about what you saw and take the average both of your scores for each question.

After touring several facilities, go to the summary sheet on page 115, and compare quality scores and other pertinent information before choosing a facility.

The nursing home tour is only part of your evaluation. Interview staff members and talk to families with loved ones living in that facility. Ask them questions from the guides on pages 147–157 and 163–166. Together, the three questionnaires will give you a complete picture of life in a particular nursing home.

Key points to remember when choosing a nursing home

- Residents should be clean, groomed, dressed, up and about, and involved in activities both indoors and outdoors.
- Staff members should be clean, groomed, friendly, active, helpful, and, most of all, caring. There must be enough staff members available to care for the residents.
- Interaction between staff members and residents should be cordial and friendly, particularly when residents are confused. Both staff members and residents should treat each other with respect and dignity.
- Listen as residents ask for help going to the bathroom. You should hear staff respond to requests and see them assist residents to a toilet.
- Facilities should be clean, uncluttered, well maintained, and well lighted.
- There should be no unpleasant odors, such as urine.
- The atmosphere should be calm, pleasant, and homelike.
- There should be a variety of activities and good food to enjoy.

Summary sheet for comparing nursing homes

Facility	Location	Contact Information	Visit Date	Quality Score	Notes

Nursing home walk-through questions

Facility ______________________ Date ____________ Time ____________

1. Were the conversations between staff and residents friendly?

1	*2*	*3*	*4*	*5*
Most were not	*Some were*	*Many were*	*Most were*	*All were*

2. When staff talked to residents, did they call them by name?

1	*2*	*3*	*4*	*5*
Most did not	*A few did*	*Some did*	*Many did*	*Most did*

3. Did residents and staff acknowledge each other and seem comfortable with each other (for example, smile, eye contact, touch, etc.)?

1	*2*	*3*	*4*	*5*
Most did not	*A few did*	*Some did*	*Many did*	*Most did*

4. Did residents and staff interact with each other in positive ways (for example, conversation, humor, touch, eye contact, etc.)?

1	*2*	*3*	*4*	*5*
Most did not	*A few did*	*Some did*	*Many did*	*Most did*

5. Did staff appear caring (compassionate, warm, kind)?

1	*2*	*3*	*4*	*5*
Most did not	*A few did*	*Some did*	*Many did*	*Most did*

6. Did staff treat residents as individuals with dignity and respect?

1	*2*	*3*	*4*	*5*
Most did not	*A few did*	*Some did*	*Many did*	*Most did*

7. Were registered nurses (RNs) visible? (Look at name badges of staff to identify RNs. May need to ask staff.)

1	*2*	*3*	*4*	*5*
Rarely seen	*Occasionally*	*Sometimes*	*Often*	*Very often*

8. Did registered nurses (RNs) seem to know the residents so that they could direct their care? (May need to ask staff.)

1	2	3	4	5
Did not seem to	*Occasionally*	*Sometimes*	*Often*	*Very often*

9. Did staff help residents with food or fluids?

1	2	3	4	5
Rarely seen	*Occasionally*	*Sometimes*	*Often*	*Very often*

10. Were residents walking or independently moving about the facility with or without assistive devices such as canes, walkers, wheelchairs?

1	2	3	4	5
Rarely seen	*Occasionally*	*Sometimes*	*Often*	*Very often*

11. Were staff helping some residents walk or move about the facility?

1	2	3	4	5
Rarely seen	*Occasionally*	*Sometimes*	*Often*	*Very often*

12. Did staff communicate with confused residents in positive ways (for example, talk, touch, sit with, etc.)?

1	2	3	4	5
Rarely seen	*Occasionally*	*Sometimes*	*Often*	*Very often*

13. Were residents dressed and clean?

1	2	3	4	5
Most were not	*Some were*	*Many were*	*Most were*	*All were*

14. Were residents well groomed (shaved, hair combed, nails clean and trimmed)?

1	2	3	4	5
Most were not	*Some were*	*Many were*	*Most were*	*All were*

15. Were odors of urine or feces noticeable in the facility?

1	2	3	4	5
Pervasive throughout	*In most areas*	*Occasionally*	*Hardly at all*	*Not at all*

16. Were other unpleasant odors noticeable in the facility?

1	2	3	4	5
Pervasive throughout	*In most areas*	*Occasionally*	*Hardly at all*	*Not at all*

17. Were hallways and common areas uncluttered?

1	2	3	4	5
Very cluttered	*Frequently cluttered*	*Somewhat cluttered*	*Neat and uncluttered*	*Very neat and uncluttered*

18. Were resident rooms, hallways, and common areas clean?

1	2	3	4	5
Dirty	*Somewhat dirty*	*More or less clean*	*Clean*	*Very clean*

19. Were buildings, grounds, and furniture in good condition?

1	2	3	4	5
Very poor condition	*Poor condition*	*Fairly good condition*	*Good condition*	*Very good condition*

20. Were the hallways well lighted?

1	2	3	4	5
Poorly lighted	*Some light but not enough*	*Moderately lighted*	*Well lighted*	*Exceptionally well lighted*

21. Were resident rooms well lighted?

1	2	3	4	5
Poorly lighted	*Some light but not enough*	*Moderately lighted*	*Well lighted*	*Exceptionally well lighted*

22. Did confused residents have a safe place to wander indoors? (May need to ask staff.)

1	2	3	4	5
No apparent safe place	*Very small*	*Small*	*Moderate*	*Large safe place*

23. Did confused residents have a safe place to wander outdoors? (May need to ask staff.)

1	2	3	4	5
No apparent safe place	*Very small*	*Small*	*Moderate*	*Large safe place*

24. Did confused residents have access to outdoor space? (May need to ask staff.)

1	2	3	4	5
No apparent access	*Occasional access with assistance*	*Some access with assistance*	*Frequent access*	*Access any time*

25. Did other residents have access to outdoor spaces? (May need to ask staff.)

1	2	3	4	5
No apparent access	*Occasional access with assistance*	*Some access with assistance*	*Frequent access*	*Access any time*

26. Were residents' rooms personalized with furniture, pictures, and other things from their past?

1	2	3	4	5
Most were not	*A few were*	*Some were*	*Many were*	*Most were*

27. Were there pets (dogs, cats, birds, etc.) and/or live plants in the facility?

1	2	3	4	5
None or rarely seen	*Occasionally*	*Sometimes*	*Often*	*Very often*

28. Were the pets and/or live plants in good condition?

1	2	3	4	5
None seen or very poor condition	*Fair condition*	*Average*	*Good*	*Very good condition*

29. Was there a homelike appearance about the facility?

1	2	3	4	5
Not at all homelike	*Somewhat*	*Moderately*	*Quite homelike*	*Very homelike*

30. Were visitors visible in the facility (family members, volunteers, community members, etc.)?

1	2	3	4	5
Rarely seen	*Occasionally*	*Sometimes*	*Often*	*Very often*

Add the scores from all 30 questions to get a total score. If two persons completed the questionnaire, add the scores together and divide them by two. The average total score is the most accurate "quality score." A score of 128 or higher suggests a good-quality nursing home. A score of 103 or lower suggests a nursing home with problems. Keep looking. Scores between these numbers are typical of most nursing homes. The higher the score, the more likely you are to be satisfied with the care and services, so make sure you have found the best you can find in your area. Driving a bit farther for good care is worth it in the long run.

Note: This Questionnaire is officially titled "OBSERVABLE INDICATORS OF NURSING HOME CARE QUALITY" VERSION 10NH (Revised – February 2005) MU MDS and Quality Research Team © 1998, 1999, 2000, 2002, 2003, 2004, 2005.

User's guide to walk-through questions for nursing homes

The following is a user's guide to explain the questions and how to judge your answers to each of the thirty questions in the walk-through for nursing homes.

1. Were the conversations between staff and residents friendly?
   It is important that staff members know the residents and communicate in a friendly manner. Did you observe staff talking to the residents about things other than resident care? For example, did the conversation focus only on medications or symptoms, or did they also discuss family, friends, the weather, and other non-care-related topics?

2. When staff talked to residents, did they call them by name?
   Staff and residents should be friends, and calling each other by name indicates a friendly relationship. Staff need to know residents well enough to recognize when they are not behaving normally, which may indicate an illness.

3. Did residents and staff acknowledge each other and seem comfortable with each other?
   Look for smiles, eye contact, touch, etc.

4. Did residents and staff interact with each other in positive ways?
   Friendly nonverbal communication—for example, smiling, making eye contact, touching, etc.—is as important as good verbal communication. Residents and staff need to be comfortable with each other. Because they interact daily, nonverbal clues can tell you a lot about how people relate. As we mentioned earlier, those friendly relations help residents stay healthy.

5. Did staff appear caring?
   Look for signs of compassion, warmth, and kindness.

6. Did staff treat residents as individuals with dignity and respect?
   Although each staff member cares for several residents, they need to know the residents and treat them as individuals with their own needs and as people worthy of their compassion and respect. You should be able to detect the staff's caring attitude toward the residents.

7. Were registered nurses (RNs) visible? (Look at name badges of staff to identify RNs. May need to ask staff.)
   If staff members are not wearing names badges, ask if any registered nurses are working on the shift you are observing.

8. Did registered nurses (RNs) seem to know the residents so that they could direct their care? (May need to ask staff.)
   Although good facilities have a lot of staff, it's the registered nurses who evaluate each resident and see that they get the care they need. Registered nurses are also trained to recognize when resident are having problems. Talk with an RN to learn more about how well he or she knows the residents. Ask him or her to describe their most challenging resident.

9. Did staff help residents with food or fluids?
   Most residents need frequent help and encouragement to take food and fluids throughout the day, not just at meal times. You should hear and see staff helping and encouraging residents to drink fluids and eat snacks or meals.

10. Were residents walking or independently moving about the facility with or without assistive devices such as canes, walkers, and wheelchairs?
    Generally, you should see some residents up and moving about the nursing home. It is important to encourage older adults to be as active as possible. Maintaining or regaining mobility is a primary goal for most residents.

11. Were staff helping some residents walk or move about the facility?
    If a resident needs help getting around, staff should be there to help.

12. Did staff communicate with confused residents in positive ways (for example, talk, touch, sit with, etc.)?
    Staff should not only be very familiar with the confused residents, they should be friends. There will be conflicts at times, but it's important to see staff communicating with confused residents. This could take the form of talking, touching, or just sitting with residents. All these indicate a friendly, caring relationship that can help staff recognize when residents are not behaving normally, which may indicate an illness.

13. Were residents dressed and clean?

14. Were residents well groomed (shaved, hair combed, nails clean and trimmed)?
    Appearance is important to all of us, regardless of our age. Some residents need help dressing and grooming themselves. Residents should appear well groomed and clean. Some residents need assistance with grooming and getting dressed. Therefore, if some residents are not well groomed, it may indicate a problem with their care.

15. Were odors of urine or feces noticeable in the facility?
    These odors should not be pervasive in the facility any more than they would be in your home. If there is a strong odor of urine or feces, it likely indicates major problems with the quality of care.

16. Were other unpleasant odors noticeable in the facility?
    When personal hygiene of residents is poor or when housekeeping or maintenance is inadequate, unpleasant odors become apparent. This should not be the case.

17. Were hallways and common areas uncluttered?
    Because nursing homes are busy places with lots of people living and working in them, some clutter is likely. However, it should not be hazardous to walk or to move a wheelchair throughout the facility.

18. Were resident rooms, hallways, and common areas clean?
    They should be clean, that is, free from dust, mold, mildew, stains on the floors or walls, etc. Floors should be clean, but they do not have to be shiny, because people with vision problems may struggle with glare.

19. Were buildings, grounds, and furniture in good condition?
    The facility is home for its residents. The building, grounds, and furniture should be in good condition. The residents should feel safe and take pride in their surroundings.

20. Were the hallways well lighted?

21. Were resident rooms well lighted?
    As we age, our eyesight declines. For residents' safety, comfort, and ability to move about the facility, it is important that they be able to see well. Lighting should be adequate for all activities with minimal glare. Natural light in all areas is important.

22. Did confused residents have a safe place to wander indoors? (May need to ask staff.)
    Confused residents need spaces to wander and be active. The spaces should be safe, and free from clutter and hazards. Ideally, staff would be located nearby in case a resident needs help, such as finding the bathroom.

23. Did confused residents have a safe place to wander outdoors? (May need to ask staff.)
    Residents need to be able to go outdoors. An ideal outdoor space for confused residents should be limited so that they can be outside but not wander into unsafe areas.

24. Did confused residents have access to outdoor space? (May need to ask staff.)
Designing safe accessible outdoor space for confused residents is challenging. Residents must not be able to wander into areas where they might be harmed. Sometimes, outdoor spaces are only available when staff members accompany residents, which limits the time residents can be outdoors.

25. Did other residents have access to outdoor spaces? (May need to ask staff.)
Many residents prefer to spend time outdoors and should be able to do so. The outdoor space should be safe, large enough to accommodate the residents, and clean and well maintained, just as the indoor space.

26. Were residents' rooms personalized with furniture, pictures, and other things from their past?
It is important that residents have personal items, because the facility is their home now.

27. Were there pets (dogs, cats, birds, etc.) and/or live plants in the facility?
Since this is home to residents, they should be allowed and encouraged to have plants or other things to make their rooms homelike. Plants should be placed throughout the facility. Many consider the presence of pets—in resident rooms and in non-food service areas—to be indicators of good quality.

28. Were the pets and/or live plants in good condition?
Any plants or pets in the facility should be in good condition. The staff is responsible for the facility's appearance and for pet care, including helping residents care for their pets.

29. Was there a homelike appearance about the facility?
The facility should look and feel like a home, not an institution. Residents should live, not just reside. Do you think residents can enjoy the facility and feel good about it? If you had a family member in the facility, would you like to come here often? If you were a resident, would you be comfortable?

30. Were visitors visible in the facility (family members, volunteers, community members, etc.)?
You should see visitors in the facility. Family members should be involved in the care of their loved ones and should be allowed and encouraged to visit. People enjoy the company of family and friends, and this should happen in the long-term care facility.

Interviewing staff in a nursing home

If you have visited a nursing home and found that it has good care, ask to interview the staff member who handles admissions. You may have to make an appointment for this interview.

Below you'll find a list of detailed interview questions about costs, payment options, staff workload, continuity of management and staff, safety information, and more. Each question includes the answer you're likely to hear if the facility is doing a good job.

The actual questionnaire (without the answers below), which appears on pages 147–157, includes space for taking notes. Copy this questionnaire and take it with you to interviews. Note that many of the issues covered here—such as helping residents adapt to life in a nursing home—are covered in greater detail in chapter 6.

Cost

- Does this nursing home accept Medicare or Medicaid payment?

  For many people, Medicare and Medicaid are important payment sources. Some nursing homes accept Medicare for short stays, so find this out up front if the stay will be brief. If you are planning a long or permanent stay and are likely to use Medicaid, then you need to find a facility that accepts Medicaid. In most cases, long-term residents pay for nursing home care until their private funds are depleted; then they apply for Medicaid. It is important to discuss the Medicaid application process with the admissions staff before admission and before private funds run out so that payment arrangements can be made in a timely fashion.

- What are the basic weekly and monthly charges?

Charges range from about $130 to $200 a day and can go much higher, depending on the services included. Prices vary from state to state, depending on Medicaid payment rates. Private pay rates vary widely, depending upon services and the type of room.

- What items are not covered in the basic charges?

  Be sure to ask about these potentially "hidden" charges so you can plan for the costs. Facilities typically have additional charges for things like:

  ❐ medications
  ❐ wheelchair
  ❐ transportation
  ❐ dental care
  ❐ beauty/barber shop
  ❐ dietary supplements
  ❐ incontinence supplies
  ❐ podiatry care
  ❐ physical, occupational, or speech therapy

- Before residents receive any service not covered by insurance, such as dental care, will staff notify them or their financial designee?

  Facilities should notify residents before rendering services for which they charge extra. If a resident designates another person to handle billing, then the facility should notify that person in advance.

- Is an advance payment required? If so, will it be returned if the resident leaves the facility?

  Some facilities require one or two months' payment in advance. They should return all or part of this if the resident leaves.

Building and rooms

- Can residents bring furniture from home?

Residents should be encouraged to bring chairs, a dresser, or other pieces of furniture, as well as pictures and other personal items that make a room or apartment more homelike.

- Can residents bring a pet?

  Some facilities encourage residents to bring a family pet, as long as the pet is sociable and the resident is able to help tend to it. In many places, the staff helps out with pet care.

- Can pets visit?

  Pet visitation should be encouraged. Be sure the pet is clean, and be mindful of proper disposal of animal waste. Also remember that other residents or family members may not enjoy animals.

- Is there adequate storage space for personal items, both in the room and in a general storage area?

  Each resident's room or apartment should have space to store personal items used frequently, plus space for a few items of off-season clothing, small seasonal decorations, and other items. Family members may want to store residents' larger belongings at home, and valuable items should always be stored at home.

- If this is a multistory building, are there adequate elevators to transport residents?

  There should be enough elevators for residents to easily get from place to place. Be sure to see for yourself that the elevators are adequate.

- Is there outdoor space for residents to enjoy?

Residents should be able to spend time outdoors. Since some people may wander, facilities should offer a safe outdoor space that prevents them from leaving the grounds.

- If smoking is allowed, how are smokers' and nonsmokers' wishes addressed?

  Many facilities have smoke-free buildings and grounds for all residents, staff, and visitors. Be sure to ask. If smoking for residents is allowed, residents should have a separate, well-ventilated area where they may safely smoke without polluting the air for others. Staff smoking areas (if allowed) should not be at a public entrance.

- How does the staff know if residents leave the building?

  In cases where residents should not leave the building without supervision, doors should have alarms to alert staff when residents leave. Some facilities use electronic devices that sound an alarm when residents pass through the doorway.

- In case of fire, does the building have a sprinkler system?

  It should have sprinklers.

- If there is a fire, how will the staff make sure the residents are safe?

  The staff should have a detailed plan and be able to explain it.

Staff

- How long have the last two administrators worked here?

It's best when administrators stay for five or more years. A facility with a stable administration is more likely to deliver better services than one with constant turnover.

- How long have the last two directors of nursing worked here?

  A director of nursing who stays for five or more years is likely to have staff and care delivery systems in place. Turnover in this position could indicate problems in delivery of care.

- How long has the current owner of the facility owned and operated it?

  Facilities with stable, long-term ownership are more likely to have staff and care delivery systems in place than those that change ownership frequently.

- Are there licensed nurses on all three shifts (day, evening, and night)?

  Although no federal regulations set staffing levels for licensed nurses (RNs or LPNs) in nursing homes, there should be a licensed nurse on-site twenty-four hours each day and an RN must be on-site a minimum of eight hours each day. Licensed practical nurses (LPNs) have about a year of education and training beyond high school.

  One national organization that advocates for residents recommends licensed nurse-to-resident ratios of 1:15 on days, 1:20 on evenings, and 1:33 on nights. Staffing varies depending on the kind of care residents need. However, licensed nurses should be working all three shifts. For more information, visit www.nursinghomeaction.org/govpolicy/51_162_472.cfm.

- Are the same registered nurses responsible for the same residents each day?

  The same registered nurses (RNs) should oversee the care for the same residents and know them well. Registered nurses, who have two to four years of college education, are responsible for knowing each resident's medical conditions and recognizing any changes that need attention. If they care for the same residents each day, they will get to know them well enough to notice these important changes. Depending upon the size of the facility, RNs should be in the facility at least eight hours each day, and many nursing homes employ RNs twenty-four hours a day. Their job is to evaluate residents' needs and see that each resident gets the care that he or she requires.

- How many residents does each nursing assistant care for on each shift?

  Nursing homes are required to employ only certified nursing assistants. To be certified, a person must have both classroom and clinical instruction and be registered by each state on a CNA list. Nursing assistants provide most of the personal care, such as helping residents eat, dress, bathe, and go to the toilet. A national resident advocacy organization recommends direct caregiver-to-resident ratios of 1:5 on days, 1:10 on evenings, and 1:15 on nights. Staffing will vary depending on recruitment, staffing policies at the facility, and the kind of care that residents need.

- Do residents have the same nursing assistants caring for them day in and day out?

When nursing assistants work with the same residents, they can get to know them, which often improves the quality of care.

- Do residents have the same housekeeper cleaning their room each time?

  It's reassuring to residents when they get to know the housecleaning staff members, who often become a source of social support.

- Does this facility use staff from a temporary employment agency?

  Temporary workers can't know the residents and their special needs, so using them consistently may cause problems. Occasional backup from an agency may be necessary, especially in some urban areas where businesses must compete for quality staff members. However, it's a red flag if a facility routinely relies on temporary workers.

- Does this facility do criminal background checks on all employees?

  All healthcare facilities should do criminal background checks. It is important that older adults not be cared for by people with criminal histories.

- How much are nursing assistants, housekeepers, and dietary staff paid? How does this compare to wages paid by other nursing homes in the community?

  Wages should be comparable to those at other local nursing homes. Workers who are fairly compensated are more likely to stay with their employers, and this often results in a higher quality of care. As you visit different facilities, you'll get a better idea of how wages compare.

- Is a registered dietitian available?

  A registered dietitian should be available to consult with the dietary staff and review meal plans.

- Are physical therapy, speech therapy, and occupational therapy available?

  All these rehabilitation therapists should be available.

- How often does your physician or other healthcare provider visit the nursing home?

  In a nursing home, healthcare providers should visit at least monthly. Residents should not have to be transported to a physician office for routine health checks.

Transition to facility life

- How does the staff help new residents adjust to the facility?

  Staff members should be able to explain how they help new residents adjust. They might use a welcome banner, new residents' teas, social service visitation, activity staff visits, and other methods to involve residents who are new to nursing home life.

- How do current residents help new residents adjust to the facility?

  They may hold a resident visitation, form a welcome committee, or come up with other ways to greet new residents and help them become part of the community.

- What are typical problems that new residents have when they come to this facility? How does the staff help them handle these problems?

The staff should be able to explain common problems that concern new residents and how they can help.

- How are residents matched as roommates? (This question may not be applicable if the facility has private rooms.)

  The staff should try to match interests, healthcare needs, ability to get along, and other characteristics. Nursing homes typically have two beds per room, though many are remodeling to add more private space.

- What happens if roommates do not get along? (This question may not be applicable if the facility has private rooms.)

  Residents should have some recourse if they cannot get along with their roommates. The staff may suggest another roommate or unit, or they might arrange a meeting between the roommates and a social worker to try to resolve the conflict.

- Do residents refer to the nursing home as "my home now"?

  Ideally, as residents adjust, they tend to refer to the nursing home as their home.

- Are there other residents here who might be interested in socializing?

  The staff should be aware of other residents who may be a good social match.

Opportunities for resident and family input

- Is there a family advisory or support group?

  There should be. Family groups can help residents and their families adjust to nursing home life.

- Do families and residents meet routinely with the administrator, director of nursing, or the other staff to discuss care and life issues?

  You should be able to meet regularly with the staff to discuss care concerns and share ideas to improve nursing home life.

- Is there a resident council?

  Many nursing homes have a resident council that meets with staff to discuss care and nursing home life.

- Is there a family council?

  Many homes have family councils that advise staff about care and quality-of-life issues to improve service.

Care issues

- What do residents usually say about the food?

  The staff should know if residents generally like the food or if they prefer certain menu offerings to others.

- What happens if a resident does not want to eat a particular meal?

  Residents should have alternatives. Ask what substitutions are available to residents each day.

- Are residents able to request special food items?

  Residents should be able to make special requests, and families should be encouraged to bring in special foods that their family member likes.

- May I taste the food and observe a meal?

  The staff should let you taste a meal prepared for the residents. Watch workers serve a meal. The food should look and smell appetizing. The ambiance in the dining room should be pleasant and appealing.

- Is there a program to help residents regain their physical abilities?

  Most facilities offer exercise or walking programs as part of basic daily care, but you should ask to be sure. If there is a separate charge, ask what residents gain from the program and how much it costs.

- Are residents assisted to the bathroom when they ask?

  They should be.

- Are toilets conveniently located for resident use?

  They should be.

- Are there grab bars and other safety devices in resident bathrooms?

  There should be.

- How does the staff help residents maintain privacy and dignity when they are given baths, toileting assistance, and other care?

  Staff members should tell you how important it is for residents to maintain privacy and dignity. They should have an orientation program in which new staff members learn these skills. When you tour the facility, you should not see residents exposed inappropriately while staff members are providing care to them.

- How long do residents typically wait until their call light is answered?

  Although staff members cannot always respond immediately, residents should not have to wait more than fifteen minutes for help. As you tour the facility, observe whether there are lots of call lights on and if staff are responding to them.

- What activities are available?

  There should be a variety of activities to interest a variety of people. Many facilities offer craft groups; music groups; shopping trips; exercise groups; small discussion groups; games like bingo and bunko; and field trips to fairs, festivals, and other community events. In addition, staff should encourage individual activities, such as reading and playing cards. There should also be activities for residents with reduced mental capacities.

- How frequently are activities offered?

  Facilities should offer activities often so that residents can socialize, explore new interests, and occupy their time. Occasional evening and weekend activities should supplement traditional midmorning and midafternoon events.

- Are religious services conducted for the residents? How often?

  Services should address the needs of people with different religions and should be frequent enough to meet residents' desires. Ask for a schedule of services.

- Can residents leave the nursing home for an outing or other leisure activity?

  There should be opportunities for occasional outings, and families should be encouraged to take loved ones out to a favorite restaurant, a wedding, family celebration, or other events.

- Do residents have the freedom to say no when they don't want something or would prefer not to do something?

  Sometimes residents do not want certain medical treatments, or they prefer not to participate in certain activities. They should have the right to say no. Treatment decisions should be discussed with the resident's doctor, family, and staff members so that everyone understands what the resident wants.

- How does the staff work to avoid using physical restraints?

  Staff should only rarely, if ever, use physical restraints, even when dealing with residents who fall frequently or exhibit difficult behaviors. You should not see residents tied to chairs or beds.

  Restraints do not prevent falls. In fact, they can cause harm by reducing walking and other body motions that people need to maintain strength. Restraints can cause additional problems like skin breakdown, strangulation, increased incontinence, and depression. When you walk through the building, you should see some beds that are very low to the floor, which helps prevent falls from the bed. You should see staff helping residents walk in the halls, which helps maintain leg muscles and balance to help prevent falls.

- How does the staff avoid the use of side rails for beds?

  Side rails do not protect residents from falling out of bed. In fact, residents risk serious injury when they attempt to get out of bed and fall over siderails. Side rails should not be used for all residents, and the decision to do so should be carefully considered.

- How does the staff help residents who are depressed?

Staff members should be able to describe a number of techniques, including talking frequently with the residents, trying to involve them in activities, and getting a psychological evaluation.

- Who is the ombudsman for this facility? Does the ombudsman visit regularly?

  Nursing homes have a consumer advocate, or ombudsman, who is a part of the official state ombudsman program. Ombudsmen investigate and attempt to resolve concerns raised by residents, and their families and friends. The staff should be able to tell you who the ombudsman is and when he or she usually comes to the facility to see residents.

Alzheimer's care

- Are there special services and activities for residents with Alzheimer's disease?

  Because residents with Alzheimer's or other dementias have special needs, facilities should offer certain services. For example, a quiet environment can minimize confusion and reduce agitated behavior. Special activities can help occupy residents and minimize wandering.

- Is the staff specially trained to care for Alzheimer's patients?

  It should be.

- Are doors secured or fitted with alarms so that residents with Alzheimer's cannot wander outside without a staff member?

  All doors leading out of the building or into areas that contain supplies or equipment should be secure. Many

Alzheimer's facilities are designed so that residents have limited spaces where they can safely wander both indoors and outdoors. In some facilities, residents can go outside into safe areas alone when they want, but staff can see them at all times. In this case, the doors to these safe areas do not need alarms.

- Do residents on the Alzheimer's unit have a safe space to enjoy outdoors?

  Many residents with Alzheimer's disease or other dementias enjoy outdoor spaces. Facilities should offer inviting outdoor spaces that provide shade in warm weather and shelter from the wind in colder weather. Residents must not be able to wander away from the building or into areas where they might be harmed.

Questions for nursing home staff

Facility ______________________ Date ______________ Time ______________

Cost

1. Does this nursing home accept Medicare or Medicaid payment?

2. What are the basic weekly and monthly charges?

3. What items are not covered in the basic charges?

❐ medications	❐ beauty/barber shop
❐ wheelchair	❐ dietary supplements
❐ transportation	❐ incontinence supplies
❐ dental care	❐ podiatry care

❐ physical, occupational, or speech therapy

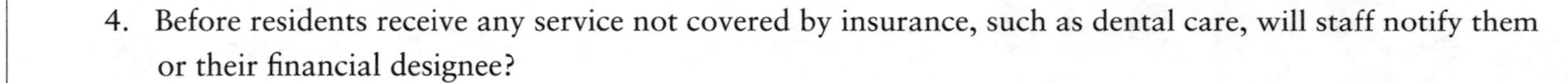

4. Before residents receive any service not covered by insurance, such as dental care, will staff notify them or their financial designee?

5. Is an advance payment required? If so, will it be returned if the resident leaves the facility?

Building and rooms

6. Can residents bring furniture from home?

7. Can residents bring a pet?

8. Can pets visit?

9. Is there adequate storage space for personal items, both in the room and in a general storage area?

10. If this is a multistory building, are there adequate elevators to transport residents?

11. Is there outdoor space for residents to enjoy?

12. If smoking is allowed, how are smokers' and nonsmokers' wishes addressed?

13. How does the staff know if residents leave the building?

14. In case of fire, does the building have a sprinkler system?

15. If there is a fire, how will the staff make sure the residents are safe?

Staff

16. How long have the last two administrators worked here?

17. How long have the last two directors of nursing worked here?

18. How long has the current owner of the facility owned and operated it?

19. Are there licensed nurses on all three shifts (day, evening, and night)?

20. Are the same registered nurses responsible for the same residents each day?

21. How many residents does each nursing assistant care for on each shift?

22. Do residents have the same nursing assistants caring for them day in and day out?

23. Do residents have the same housekeeper cleaning their room each time?

24. Does this facility use staff from a temporary employment agency?

25. Does this facility do criminal background checks on all employees?

26. How much are nursing assistants, housekeepers, and dietary staff paid? How does this compare to wages paid by other nursing homes in the community?

27. Is a registered dietitian available?

28. Are physical therapy, speech therapy, and occupational therapy available?

29. How often does your physician or other healthcare provider visit the nursing home?

Transition to facility life

30. How does the staff help new residents adjust to the facility?

31. How do current residents help new residents adjust to the facility?

32. What are typical problems that new residents have when they come to this facility? How does the staff help them handle these problems?

33. How are residents matched as roommates? (Does not apply if private rooms.)

34. What happens if roommates do not get along? (Does not apply if private rooms.)

35. Do residents refer to the nursing home as “my home now”?

36. Are there other residents here who might be interested in socializing?

Opportunities for resident and family input

37. Is there a family advisory or support group?

38. Do families and residents meet routinely with the administrator, director of nursing, or the other staff to discuss care and life issues?

39. Is there a resident council?

40. Is there a family council?

Care issues

41. What do residents usually say about the food?

42. What happens if a resident does not want to eat a particular meal?

43. Are residents able to request special food items?

44. May I taste the food and observe a meal?

45. Is there a program to help residents regain their physical abilities?

46. Are residents assisted to the bathroom when they ask?

47. Are toilets conveniently located for resident use?

48. Are there grab bars and other safety devices in resident bathrooms?

49. How does the staff help residents maintain privacy and dignity when they are given baths, toileting assistance, and other care?

50. How long do residents typically wait until their call light is answered?

51. What activities are available?

52. How frequently are activities offered?

53. Are religious services conducted for the residents? How often?

54. Can residents leave the nursing home for an outing or other leisure activity?

55. Do residents have the freedom to say no when they don't want something or would prefer not to do something?

56. How does the staff work to avoid using physical restraints?

57. How does the staff avoid the use of side rails for beds?

58. How does the staff help residents who are depressed?

59. Who is the ombudsman for this facility? Does the ombudsman visit regularly?

Alzheimer's care

60. Are there special services and activities for residents with Alzheimer's disease?

61. Is the staff specially trained to care for Alzheimer's patients?

62. Are doors secured or fitted with alarms so that residents cannot wander outside without a staff member?

63. Do residents on the Alzheimer's unit have a safe space to enjoy outdoors?

Interviewing families of residents in a nursing home

When you think you've found a nursing home that's a good fit, we recommend interviewing family members of some residents. Strike up conversations with other visitors as you tour the facility. Tell them what you are considering, and ask if they'd be willing to talk about their experiences.

This chapter contains key questions to help you glean others' impressions of a facility's staff and policies. As in chapter 4, we provide a sample of a "good" answer for each question.

The actual questionnaire (without the answers below) is on pages 163–166. Make as many copies as you need, and use a new copy for each interview. Feel free to ask your own questions as well.

- Does your loved one seem to enjoy certain parts of the day (events, mealtimes, etc.), every day?

  The resident should. Ask family members for examples.

- Do staff treat your loved one with respect and courtesy?

  They should.

- Are residents encouraged to be as independent as possible?

  They should be. Ask for examples. Residents should strive for independence, though abilities differ.

- How often do you visit?

  Responses will vary. Try to get a sense of whether people feel they must visit to make sure the staff is taking care of their loved one. Also, try to learn whether they're afraid to leave their family member alone for some reason.

- Is the staff positive toward your visits?

  They should be. If not, ask the family why.

- Is there a call light system that your loved one can use? Are staff members responsive to the lights and other requests for care?

  Although every nursing home should have a reliable call system, the staff cannot respond to each request immediately (just as families cannot do in day-to-day living). However, residents should not have to wait more than fifteen minutes when they request help, especially if they need to use the toilet. The staff should be responsive and meet needs in a timely fashion.

- Do the same staff members regularly care for your loved one?

  The more they do, the better the care is likely to be.

- Do staff members seem to know your loved one as a person? Are they able to talk to your loved one about details of his or her life?

  The staff should know the residents well, and they should be receptive to residents who try to share details of their lives.

- Does the staff know what kind of care your loved one needs?

  They should.

- Do you think the staff takes proper care of your loved one?

  Although few family members are experts in nursing home care, observation and intuition should tell them that their loved one is well cared for.

- Has your loved one ever complained of not being treated well?

If so, ask them to tell you the story. Did the staff seem to be deliberately mistreating the resident? That should not be the case.

- Do you think the staff listens to you?

  Families should feel that staff members listen, and they should be able to give you an example or two to support this perception.

- Does your loved one feel like this is home now?

  That is an ideal situation, but remember that it can take time. Find out how long this person has been a resident. Generally, most residents adjust to the move in a few weeks or months.

- Do staff members encourage residents to remain continent?

  They should. Staff members should take residents to the bathroom when they ask to go. Families should never hear the staff say, "You have a diaper on, so it is okay to go ahead and go."

- Are residents and families involved in care planning?

  The staff should ask family members for input, then incorporate their suggestions into a written care plan. Care-plan meetings are scheduled to review and discuss the care provided by the staff for each resident. Residents and family members should be invited and encouraged to participate in routine care-plan meetings and care planning in general.

- Does the staff follow up on issues raised in care-plan meetings?

Family members should be able to offer an example or two of how the staff followed through on issues.

- Is your loved one fearful of complaining?

  Residents should be able to state reasonable complaints without fear. Fearfulness is common among people who feel vulnerable, so staff should help residents feel safe and able to voice complaints.

- If you complain, how does the staff deal with your complaints?

  Try to get a sense of the family member's complaint, how they broached it, and how the staff responded.

- Have you been concerned about personal items being lost or misplaced?

  This may happen occasionally, but it should not be common. Personal items can be difficult to keep track of, so mark them clearly to help staff members put them back where they belong. Store expensive items, such as heirloom jewelry, at home. Provide costume jewelry for a loved one to wear. If an item is misplaced, you will not have lost a family keepsake.

- If your loved one is injured or becomes ill, does the staff contact you quickly?

  They should.

- Does your loved one feel safe and secure in this facility?

  He or she should.

- Have you ever been concerned about your loved one's safety?

Although nursing homes are not risk free, listen for excessive concern. Ask what the family knows about security precautions at the nursing home and their effectiveness.

- Knowing what you know now, if you had to choose a nursing home today, would you still select this one?

  If the family is satisfied with the care and services, they would.

Questions for family members of residents in a nursing home

Facility ____________ Name ____________ Date ________ Time ________

1. Does your loved one seem to enjoy certain parts of the day (events, mealtimes, etc.), every day?

2. Do staff treat your loved one with respect and courtesy?

3. Are residents encouraged to be as independent as possible?

4. How often do you visit?

5. Is the staff positive toward your visits?

6. Is there a call light system that your loved one can use? Are staff members responsive to the lights and other requests for care?

7. Do the same staff members regularly care for your loved one?

8. Do staff members seem to know your loved one as a person? Are they able to talk to your loved one about details of his or her life?

9. Does the staff know what kind of care your loved one needs?

10. Do you think the staff takes proper care of your loved one?

11. Has your loved one ever complained of not being treated well?

12. Do you think the staff listens to you?

13. Does your loved one feel like this is home now?

14. Do staff members encourage residents to remain continent?

15. Are residents and families involved in care planning?

16. Does the staff follow up on issues raised in care-plan meetings?

17. Is your loved one fearful of complaining?

18. If you complain, how does the staff deal with your complaints?

19. Have you been concerned about personal items being lost or misplaced?

20. If your loved one is injured or becomes ill, does the staff contact you quickly?

21. Does your loved one feel safe and secure in this facility?

22. Have you ever been concerned about your loved one's safety?

23. Knowing what you know now, if you had to choose a nursing home today, would you still select this one?

Who will pay for nursing home care?

The cost of nursing home care can run from $50,000 to $80,000 a year—a staggering amount for most people. But don't lose heart. Financing alternatives do exist. The four basic options are Medicaid, Medicare, long-term care insurance, and personal funds. In the following pages, we describe these options in broad terms. However, the rules and regulations are constantly changing, and they vary from state to state, so ask your nursing home social worker for help sorting through the details.

Medicaid

The vast majority of nursing homes participate in the Medicaid program, a federally mandated, state-sponsored program that helps many people who could not otherwise afford to pay for medical care. In fact, Medicaid pays 60 percent of all nursing home bills nationwide. In a few states, Medicaid may also pay for other long-term care options, including assisted living or residential care, board-and-care homes, and some community-based services.

If you think you might use Medicaid to pay for nursing home care—whether now or in the future—you must:

1. Be sure the nursing home you choose is certified by Medicaid.
2. Check with the nursing home staff to be certain the resident needs the kind of care that the nursing home delivers. (Medicaid requires preadmission screenings to make sure residents need the kind of care they'll receive.)
3. Find out if the resident will qualify for Medicaid. (The nursing home social worker will help you through the process and answer any questions you may have.)

To qualify for Medicaid, most people are required to contribute a substantial amount of their income—typically a Social Security check—before the state will pick up the balance. Widowed and unmarried people must "spend down" their assets before coverage starts.

This means they must sell their home unless they can establish that they will probably return to it. For individuals who have a spouse living at home, many assets, including the residence and some income, are exempt. So, a resident's spouse could keep the home, car, clothing, and some other assets such as stocks, bonds, pension income, savings, and bank accounts, although this can vary widely by state. Work closely with the nursing home staff to help you get the paperwork in order for Medicaid and connect you with the Medicaid staff in your state so that you comply with the regulations. Expect to spend some time processing paperwork and working with your bank and insurance companies to qualify for Medicaid.

Some attorneys specialize in arranging assets in a way that works to a person's advantage and lets him or her qualify for Medicaid. If you or your loved one are interested in arranging your assets, find an attorney who specializes in estate planning. Remember, laws vary from state to state. Penalties for divesting assets in an attempt to qualify for Medicaid are high, and you or your loved one could be disqualified from receiving any future Medicaid assistance. Always consult an attorney when handling assets, and be sure you know the laws in your state.

Medicare

Medicare, a federal insurance program, will usually cover short-term stays in a nursing home. Although most people qualify for Medicare coverage at age sixty-five, not all nursing homes are Medicare-certified. To receive Medicare payment, a nursing home must complete a special certification process. (Note that a facility's Medicare certification is not a guarantee of good-quality care.)

Medicare will cover nursing home care only under certain conditions. Typically, coverage follows hospitalization. If the resident qualifies, Medicare will pay the nursing home bill for the first twenty days. After that, a daily copayment is required. (Many supplemental Medicare insurance policies will pay for all or most of this copayment.) The maximum number of days covered is usually one hundred. However, there are regulations that measure continued progress of the rehabilitation for each person using Medicare in a nursing home. So, if progress cannot be substantiated, Medicare will stop payment. When coverage runs out or progress cannot be substantiated, the resident must switch to Medicaid or private payment, according to his or her financial situation.

As a general rule, if you anticipate a short nursing home stay after a hospitalization, you should look for a Medicare-certified nursing home. If you anticipate a long-term or permanent stay, then Medicare certification is not an important feature to look for.

Medicare benefits are extremely complicated, and you will need help from the nursing home billing staff to determine exactly what will be paid for. Be sure to ask about costs of services not covered so that you can be prepared to pay those when needed or wanted.

Once admitted to the nursing home, the pharmacist who works with the facility may review your Medicare part D program. You may need to switch programs to best cover your medications now that you are living in a nursing home.

Long-term care insurance

Long-term care insurance may pay for some or all of a resident's nursing home care, depending upon the coverage purchased. Typically, there are limits on the daily payments and the duration of coverage. (For example, a policy might pay $130 per day for three years.) Some long-term care insurance will cover homecare services, but, again, limitations will vary from policy to policy.

For most people, the premiums for long-term care insurance are only affordable if they bought their policy in their fifties or sixties. Generally, when people in their seventies decide to buy long-term care insurance, the cost is quite high. More long-term care insurance options are becoming available, especially in group plans. Sometimes group plans allow parents or grandparents of an employee to participate; check with family members to see if this is an option for you or your loved ones.

If you choose to buy long-term care insurance, do your homework. Make sure the company is reputable and financially sound. Many people have been victimized by dishonest companies, and some states are now vigorously regulating the sale of these policies. You might want to check with your local Area Agency on Aging or Senior Center, which likely provides assistance, advice, and advocacy for older adults seeking insurance.

In general, long-term care insurance is appropriate for people who have significant assets they want to protect. Typical policies have a three- to six-month waiting period before they begin to pay for nursing home care. If the resident exhausts all his or her assets during this period, he or she would probably qualify for Medicaid. In this case, the insurance premiums would be a waste of money.

Personal funds

If you or your loved one are fortunate enough to have the resources to pay for an extended or permanent stay in a nursing home, you will have your pick of facilities, services, and accommodations.

Faith communities, fraternal organizations, and some for-profit companies will sometimes sponsor upscale facilities that cater to private-pay residents. There are relatively few of these facilities, but they tend to provide more care options (at a higher cost) since they have fewer financial constraints.

Remember, if the resident outlives his or her assets and the nursing home is not Medicaid-certified, then the resident will have to move to a Medicaid-certified facility.

How to survive the paperwork

Before receiving Medicaid or other public assistance, applicants must show that they qualify. They will be asked to share details about life insurance policies and beneficiaries, income tax records, retirement benefits, and other financial information. They may also need to submit a physician-verified document describing their care needs. The amount of paperwork involved can be intimidating, so it's best to ask up front for a complete list of the documents required. Ask for help from the nursing home social worker or billing staff to guide you through the paperwork.

Also, be sure the nursing home has a copy of the resident's living will and durable power of attorney for healthcare. If these don't exist, it's best to create them so that the resident's wishes will be carried out in the event of future illness or injury.

Case examples of different payment options for nursing home care

Mr. and Mrs. Brown

Mr. Brown has been diagnosed with dementia and other chronic illnesses, and his health has declined for several years. His wife of fifty years had been caring for him, but her own health was challenged by her daily and nightly caregiving responsibilities. Finally, their physician recommended nursing home care for Mr. Brown.

The admissions staff at the nursing home, along with the county aging service that approves Medicaid applications, helped Mrs. Brown arrange payment for her husband's nursing home care. She retained ownership of their home, car, personal effects, and a portion of their life savings. Mr. Brown's portion purchased prepaid burial services and his initial care in the nursing home. When these funds are gone, Medicaid will take over. Mrs. Brown is relieved—her husband now has twenty-four-hour care, and her home is still her home.

Mrs. Grant

Mrs. Grant fell in her home and fractured her right hip. She was hospitalized, and surgeons repaired her injuries. After a few days, her physician suggested that a short stay in a nursing home would help her finish rehabilitation so that she could return home.

Mrs. Grant had Medicare coverage and a supplemental insurance policy. Her son and daughter-in-law located a good nursing home in their community—it scored well on the walk-through, and they were satisfied with the responses they received during the staff and family interviews. In addition, the home was certified to accept Medicare payment. Mrs. Grant received care and rehabilitation services for four weeks, then returned home. Medicare and her supplemental insurance paid most of the charges. Mrs. Grant paid some additional charges, including for beauty shop and podiatry services.

Ms. Lewis

Ms. Lewis is a forty-five-year-old woman who had an active career in publishing. During the past five years she developed severe multiple sclerosis. She needs help in meeting her physical needs. Her mother and father first helped her stay at her own home. Then she stayed with them for a year with the help of in-home health services. As Ms. Lewis continued to need more care, she and her family decided to look for a good nursing home. They found one in a small town about forty miles from where Ms. Lewis used to work. The home accepts only private-pay residents, so Ms. Lewis and her parents are planning to pay for the services out of her investment savings and, if necessary, out of their own investments. They have more than enough assets to cover the cost of care for many years to come.

CHAPTER SIX

Making It Work

Once you have found high-quality long-term care (senior housing, assisted living, or a nursing home) and gone through the admissions and moving process, you and your entire family will have a period of adjustment. During this time, you will need to shift your attention to making life in a new "home" the best it can be for the new resident.

From the start, it's important to get involved with life in the facility, activities, and, in the case of nursing homes, care planning. You must also focus on developing relationships with the staff, making the staff your allies, communicating expectations clearly, and advocating for the best care possible.

What does this move mean?

When a person moves into long-term care, particularly to a nursing home, it takes time for the new resident and his or her family to grieve for what has been lost and to adjust to a different life. Sometimes, family members may have to assume new roles. They might feel guilt and remorse, thinking they should have somehow prevented the need for the move. Residents and family members may suddenly have an acute awareness of their own mortality.

Some seniors are proactive. They "take the bull by the horns" and make decisions for themselves and adapt to long-term care because they do not want to burden family members. In other cases, families or healthcare providers may force a decision because the senior is unable or unwilling to come to terms with physical or mental decline. Regardless of the circumstances, leaving one's own residence can be a painful and difficult event that, to some, signifies a loss of independence. To others, the move signifies just another adjustment in life.

It is normal for both the resident and the family to feel many emotions during this time. In fact, even those who care for the resident will go through an adjustment period as they get to know a new resident and family and learn how best to help them.

The resident adjusts

People moving into long-term care facilities need to adjust to living in a new place. When moving into senior housing or assisted living, be sure the resident brings favorite furniture and significant objects. On a smaller scale, the same holds true for moving into a nursing home.

Some people find themselves needing nursing home care when they least expect it. The move often follows a hospitalization, when an individual feels especially unprepared to undertake such an important life event. If a senior is moving into a nursing home from a hospital, family members and hospital staff can help you find a good place. Trust others to be your eyes and ears, but always remember that the important decisions are still yours to make.

A resident may feel many things before and during the relocation to the nursing home or other long-term care setting. Anger, fear, frustration, and loneliness are common—as are a sense of relief and a feeling of safety. Allow the senior to feel these emotions, but recognize that other loved ones are working through emotions of their own.

Give everyone some time to adjust, and try to be patient with yourself and others. You can meet this challenge. Remember a challenge in your past and reflect on how you worked your way through it.

The resident should try activities in his or her new home. The senior can always decide later not to participate. And make sure the resident's room is decorated with personal possessions. Have family or friends bring in a favorite quilt, some favorite pictures, and other things that are special to the person. Move in favorite items of furniture that will fit in the room or apartment if the resident will be in the facility for an extended period of time.

Let staff members know the senior's preferences. For example, tell them when the resident prefers to go to bed at night and whether he or she prefers to bathe or shower in the morning or the evening. Many facilities will try very hard to plan care to meet personal preferences.

The senior should try to spend at least some part of every day doing something he or she would have done at home. For example, read, pray, pet the facility cat, or watch a favorite television program. This will help to normalize the days and ease the adjustment to living in a nursing home, senior housing, or assisted living.

Encourage the senior to strike up conversations with staff, other residents, and visitors. It is likely he or she will find others who share interests or find people with whom to establish friendships. It is surprising how people in a long-term care facility are somehow connected to most of the people who live in the community. Reach out and make a new friend or connect with others you may have known in the past.

> *"It was hard for me to make this move, but this is home now, and I like it. I have my own room. I could never share a room with someone, so I am lucky to have my own room. The staff helps me and the food is good. You will not believe it, but one of the other people who lives here is someone I worked with years ago. And one of the staff is a relative of one of my neighbors from my hometown. Small world."*

The family adjusts

Most people never think that their loved ones, no matter how old or frail, will ever have to leave their home. Somehow, we think our family will never age, never need long-term care, and never need a nursing home. However, when the need for nursing home care becomes apparent, family members are often frustrated that somehow they did not prevent this from happening, or that they somehow should do more. In many cases, family caregivers or friends are unable to perform all the necessary care. Then, decisions are necessary to find and accept help with care giving. At first that may mean accepting service providers coming to a person's home, but eventually it may mean long-term care, particularly nursing home care.

If your loved one has entered a nursing home, expect to feel some grief. You may feel you've let your loved one down. In addition, your family house, the scene of your childhood, may be gone now, and things will never be the same.

As you help your loved one make the transition, it is important to take care of yourself, too. If you have been the primary caregiver until now, you may be very tired. Feelings may be close to the surface. Just knowing that this is normal will help you cope.

If your family member resisted the move to the nursing home, you may feel guilt about pushing for the transition. Your loved one may show his or her anger by placing unreasonable demands on your time and attention. It's important to try to meet your family member's needs without putting yourself in impossible situations. So, plan a reasonable visiting schedule and stick to it. If you have siblings, try to alternate visits so that your loved one has plenty of company. This may be the time to ask for help from your friends as well.

Visits needn't be long. Just dropping in at different times on different days may satisfy your loved one and allow you to see that things are going fine. Give yourself some time to rest and give your loved one time and support to adjust to living in a nursing home. Notice that we say "living" in a nursing home. There is life and living in long-term care, particularly in those places with good-quality care.

With a loved one living in a nursing home or assisted living, you now have help. You can rest, renew relationships, and try to envision the future. Your family member will be safe when you're not there. Others are there to help—to make sure your loved one has food, activities, company, and healthcare.

As for your own integration into life in long-term care, family members may want to consider volunteering to help with activities, such as fund-raising events, crafts, a book club, discussion groups, or sing-alongs. As a volunteer, you will meet family members of other residents and will likely find you have many things in common, including this adjustment process. Work with staff members to help them give your family member the best possible care. Help your loved one get involved in life in the facility, make new friends, renew old interests, and be as independent as possible.

> *"My husband and I decided to become volunteers. You really get to know the staff and residents well that way. And it makes us feel better knowing that we're helping the residents. My husband enjoys playing cards with a group of the residents each week, and I help with book club discussions. We have new interests now and enjoy the other residents and getting to know their families."*

Pick up your life again. If, before the move, you had been dedicating a great deal of time and energy to helping your loved one live at home, the new arrangement should give you much-needed time to reconnect with your family and friends. This is the time to be with other people you love. Enjoy the activities that you simply didn't have time for before. And rest. Shed the feelings of exhaustion that may have become so common they felt normal to you. Take the time to care for yourself and then take some time to get involved in the lives of the residents.

Overcoming the awkwardness of first visits

It may seem odd, but visitors often don't know what to do when they call on someone, even a close family member, in a long-term care facility or senior housing. It may help to bring along "props" to make everyone more comfortable and to have something to talk about. Sometimes a prop like family photos or other interesting photos—large ones if eyesight is poor—can help spark conversation and overcome any awkwardness. Another idea for a prop is to bring something you found at home or a rummage sale that reminds you of your loved one's past.

Sometimes older people experience depression or Alzheimer's disease. If your family member is depressed or confused, conversation may be difficult, so try bringing seasonal foods, such as oranges or strawberries. Savor the fruit together, and reminisce about fruits from different seasons. Bring some favorite cookies or another familiar treat to enjoy together and talk about other times you have enjoyed those together.

> "*My dad can't talk with me anymore—he has severe dementia. But he loves strawberries. I try to find the biggest ones to bring when I visit. We sit, and I talk about the kids and work, and we eat strawberries together. He seems content. It makes me feel better; even though he can't talk to me I talk to him, and we enjoy strawberries together.*"

Bring along a favorite pet. Dogs, cats, and other animals really spark reactions from residents. Encourage your loved one to stroke the animal. Talk about other animals from the past. Bring children along, too, as well as toys for them to play with. Some assisted-living facilities and nursing homes have an area for children to play in while you visit with your family member. Talk about the things the children are doing, or broaden the conversation to other children in the family, as well as the things you and your loved one did as children. If the facility has equipment for viewing videos or DVDs, bring along a favorite movie or videos of family parties, graduations, and weddings.

> *"We bring the kids and their toys—it makes our visits easier. Mom still gets upset at times, but my kids make her smile. They love to come here and see everyone. I make sure they have toys to keep them somewhat occupied, but before you know it they're in the activity room with other residents, the dog that lives here, and the activities staff."*

One woman we know lives far from the assisted-living facility where her father now lives. She writes him several large-type letters a week. In one short letter, she mentioned that the weather had been good and the farmers were out planting corn. She went on to say, "Remember, Dad, how you always planted our corn in the straightest rows in the county?" Her father likes to get mail, and staff members enjoy reading the letters to him. His daughter includes information from his past so that the staff will continue to learn about him and always have something new to talk with him about.

Visits are about being with another person. Even if a family member is not able to converse, there are other fine ways to spend time together. Try walking with the resident or wheeling him or her about the home to visit other areas. Or, try a hand massage. People need and want to be touched, and hand massages are particularly soothing for many people. Ask other families and staff members for ideas that might make your visits more meaningful.

Warning signs to watch for

Sometimes, when people move to a new location, the stress of moving and settling in can result in depression. It is important to recognize signs of depression and talk to facility staff about what you are seeing. Some people who are depressed cry, are unreasonably angry with themselves and others, withdraw or refuse to become active in facility life, lose their appetite and lose weight, have a change in sleep or activity patterns, talk a lot about physical illness, and repetitively ask questions or complain. Allow your loved one time to adjust, but discuss the situation with facility staff, especially nurses, social workers, and activity staff.

When should you ask about calling in a psychiatrist or other mental health professional? If your loved one is losing weight or doesn't seem to be settling in after several weeks, it may be time to call for this additional help. The healthcare provider might prescribe an antidepressant medication; however, this can take two to four weeks to work effectively, so it is best not to linger over the decision to discuss this with your healthcare provider. Sometimes, moving to a nursing home causes residents to have a period of confusion, but this should pass as they adjust to the new environment.

Adjustment can best be gauged by whether a resident does some of the same things he or she did before moving to the long-term care facility. For example, if your loved one is an active person who has always gotten involved with others, is he or she getting to know the other residents? If your loved one has always been a quiet reader, is he or she beginning to read again? As a rule of thumb, people who were quite social before moving into senior housing, assisted living, or nursing homes, are the quickest to meet others and become involved in activities. These people may have an easier time adjusting.

How to respond to confusion

If your loved one suffers from Alzheimer's disease or another related dementia, moving to assisted living or a nursing home may increase their confusion. Because agitated behavior will commonly occur around the same time each day, it's important for the staff to get to know your resident's schedule. Any behavior patterns you noticed at home will most likely occur in the nursing home, too. The more information you can give the staff, the better. For example, a woman who had many children or grandchildren may begin to look for kids coming home from school at 3:30 p.m. A man who owned a dairy farm may awaken at 5 a.m. to milk the cows. Be sure staff members are aware of such behaviors so that they can plan interventions to keep your loved one busy during times of confusion.

When speaking with a confused resident, we recommend using a validation and distraction technique, rather than attempting to reorient the person. For example, when a man asks to talk with his wife who has been dead for several years, ask him to tell you about her. What was she like, what did she like to do, what did she look like? While talking about his wife, the man may remember for himself that she is dead, or he may go on to another activity without becoming agitated and upset. Do not try to reorient the man by telling him that his wife died years ago and he cannot speak to her. Confronting him may cause an agitated, angry, or bitter grief response. Discuss what she was like and move on to another topic. This is a much kinder and more effective approach for dealing with confusion.

Often, nursing homes have special care units for people with Alzheimer's disease or other types of dementia. These units should have staff members who are specially trained to deal with confused residents. There should be a safe place to wander both indoors and outdoors, as well as a variety of activities. Similarly, some assisted-living facilities specialize in caring for those with Alzheimer's. The facilities are designed to help each resident remain as independent as possible for as long as possible and engage them in activities they can enjoy. This is particularly true for those long-term care facilities offering good-quality care.

The benefits of a family council

If a family council or other family group doesn't yet exist in the long-term care facility or senior housing, help start one. Family groups serve two important functions: to help families get to know one another, and to identify problems affecting the residents. Through a family group, you and your loved one will meet other families and residents, and you will have more to talk about as you make new friends. When families come together, they can make the facility even better.

Family groups can work with staff members to seek constructive and innovative solutions to any problems that arise. In fact, families often have concerns that the staff, nurses, or administrator need to know about—housekeeping problems, malfunctioning machinery, nursing care that just doesn't seem right. Most administrators and nurses want to know about problems like these. Approaching such concerns as a group can be a faster, more effective way to bring about change.

A word about laundry

One of the great nursing home (and in some cases, assisted living) mysteries involves personal laundry. Clothes disappear. Clothes are misplaced. Clothes are ruined. Plus, it takes more time than you ever imagined possible for clothes to come back from the laundry.

Some tips: Find out how long it takes for the facility to wash laundry and return it to residents' rooms, and then do some math. Let's say the turnaround is four days. If your family member is incontinent, he or she may need two to four changes of clothes each day. So, you'll need to provide at least eight to sixteen changes of clothes. Assuming one or two episodes of incontinence per night, you will need four to eight changes of nightclothes. By providing enough clothes, you'll save yourself time and frustration.

Should you choose to do your loved one's laundry, post signs to that effect in his or her room and provide a container for the dirty clothes. Some facilities have washers and dryers for residents to use. Doing laundry together can be a good activity when visiting and can avoid delays caused by sending clothing to a central laundry.

No matter who does the laundry, be sure to clearly mark each item with the resident's name and room number. That way, if clothing is moved or misplaced, it will stand a better chance of finding its way back to the right room. If you choose to have laundry washed in the facility's central laundry, bear in mind that the commercial washers and dryers tend to wear out clothing faster than home washing, so you may need to replace clothes more often than usual.

Choose cheerful, comfortable clothing that is not only washable but also easy to put on and take off. Although your loved one may never have worn fleece clothes before, they are warm, comfortable, and usually easy to get on and off. Extra socks and underwear are always needed, and comfortable, well-fitting shoes are essential to prevent tripping. Try sneakers with Velcro closures—they are easy to get on and off, and they fit snugly on the feet.

Working with long-term care staff

Remember: without staff, nothing is possible. To get the best from senior housing, assisted living, or a nursing home, you need to work closely with staff members. Most large assisted-living facilities or nursing homes have many healthcare workers and other service providers caring for residents. Smaller assisted-living facilities and senior housing are likely to have fewer staff with more "universal" workers, who help residents with personal care as well as other tasks like cooking or serving meals, and housekeeping chores, too.

Kinds of staff

Senior housing usually has a housing manager or administrator who handles day-to-day administrative work and helps people who are considering moving to senior housing. There is usually a worker who maintains the building and makes repairs in apartments as people move in and out of the building. Any personal care services for residents are typically provided by staff of a home health agency. There may be staff to handle cooking and dining tasks as well as housekeeping staff who clean common areas of the building; they may provide weekly or periodic housekeeping in apartments.

Assisted-living facilities have a lead manager and nursing homes have a lead administrator to oversee the entire operation of the facility; this person is responsible for all the residents and the staff. The administrator-manager is licensed by the state to ensure that he or she understands the laws and regulations governing assisted-living facilities and nursing homes, as well as the basics of geriatric care. Nursing homes have a director of nursing and assisted-living facilities have a nurse manager. In nursing homes, the director of nursing is an RN, while in assisted living, the nurse manager may be a licensed practical nurse. The director of nursing or nurse manager oversees resident care and supervises all nurses, nursing assistants, and other care providers.

In nursing homes and assisted-living facilities, nursing assistants give most of the direct care. Some assisted-living nursing assistants learn on the job and others are certified as required in nursing homes after attending a minimum of 120 hours of classes. Nursing assistants provide most of the "hands-on" care. Under the direction of licensed nurses, they assist residents with bathing, toileting, feeding, and more. Nursing assistants who work in a Medicare- or Medicaid-certified nursing home are required to be certified.

Registered nurses (RNs) have a minimum of two to four years' college education in nursing. They assess each resident, treat common medical problems, and see that every resident gets the care he or she needs. Licensed practical nurses (LPNs) and licensed vocational nurses (LVNs) have about a year of post–high school education in basic nursing care. They are licensed to provide basic care and medical treatment to older adults.

A key reason that people move into nursing homes is to have professionals monitor illnesses that may have become too complex or unstable for them or for their family members to manage at home. It may be that their chronic illnesses need continuous assessment and managing by RNs, or their care directed for more comfort as they approach the end of life. Sometimes end-of-life care is best managed with twenty-four-hour staff, with RNs to help with pain management and nursing assistants to help with personal care needs.

Another key reason that people move into nursing homes is for rehabilitation. When older people are hospitalized for serious illnesses or injuries, they may need to spend some rehabilitation time in a nursing home. Rehabilitation helps them regain functions such as walking and the ability to care for themselves, and helps them gain strength to once again manage at home. Many nursing home residents receive rehabilitation so that they can live again at home on their own.

Other direct-care staff people include social workers, activities directors, and dietary managers. Typically, a social worker will help new residents and their families through the admissions process. Social workers also help residents and families adjust to nursing home life, and they often arrange community services, such as Meals on Wheels, for people who plan to return home after their nursing home stay.

The activities director not only organizes individual and group activities but also recruits volunteers. Volunteers are essential to quality care—they read letters, assist with activities, and help keep residents' lives rich and full.

> *"The activities person is a jewel. She can get my dad to do things I never thought he'd be willing to do."*

The dietary director's job is to ensure that meals are tasty and nutritious, varied, and prepared the way the residents like them. The dietary director works with a dietitian to create balanced meals and address special dietary needs. He or she directs the dietary department, orders food and supplies, and oversees the cooks and other kitchen staff members during meal preparation.

Dietitians, pharmacists, and therapists also provide direct care, whether they are permanent staff members or independent contractors. Dietitians assess special dietary needs and help residents regain or maintain a healthy body weight. Pharmacists ensure that the medications residents take are appropriate for their conditions. Physical, occupational, and speech therapists help residents regain functions lost due to illness or injury.

Finally, most long-term care facilities have business office staff to handle residents' accounts, billing, insurance, payroll records, and employee's paychecks. There may be one or several maintenance workers on staff to keep the heating, air-conditioning, water, power, and building in good order, and to help residents with television hookups and room repairs. Housekeepers are assigned to all residents' living units.

Educate staff members about the resident

Long-term care staff members are just like anybody else—they tend to like people more as they get to know them better. As professionals, staff members should spend time getting to know each resident. You can help foster this relationship by telling the staff about key life details. For instance, what did you or your loved one enjoy before coming to live in the facility? What activities would be most enjoyable now? The more staff members know and understand about the people in their care, the easier it is for them to treat their residents with dignity and kindness.

Because nursing assistants provide most of the direct care, make a point of finding those assistants who have been there awhile and get to know them well. In many places, nursing assistants may move frequently from job to job, so you'll need to continuously educate new staff members. Try to get to know them and work with them.

> *"It really helped to get to know the nursing assistants and the nurses well. I don't know what I would do without them. They have helped me so much with my mom."*

A memory collage or a memory box can help the staff and other residents get to know you or your family member as a person—and both items are good for decorating a room. Include items that reflect earlier life. For example, a housewife and mother may include examples of needlework, a poem, pictures of her family, or a picture of herself as a young woman. A former firefighter may want to include citations for bravery, pictures of the crew, pictures of his family, or a miniature of his fire hat.

Make staff members your allies

Communicating with the staff is vital to keeping the quality of care as high as possible. We recommend a tried-and-true method of communication: the Golden Rule. Treat others as you would want to be treated. As you get to know the staff, focus on building relationships that are strong, open, and respectful.

Naturally, problems will develop and the staff may well underestimate how much these difficulties disturb you. It's best to raise your concerns as problems occur. Be pleasant and respectful when speaking with the staff. Clearly identify your concerns in "I" words. For example, "I would appreciate it if you called me Mrs. Smith, not Ida. I have always been a very proper woman and I am not comfortable with people calling me by my first name." Or, "I noticed that Dad needs a haircut. When is he scheduled for the barber? He was always so meticulous about his hair." Of course, it's equally important to acknowledge when staff members are doing a good job: "I noticed how much extra care you took in explaining things to my mother. I really appreciate that. It will help her feel secure."

On occasion, the staff might behave in a way that makes you angry. Your strong reaction may be justified, but, unless you or your loved one are in danger, it is best not to confront others when you are angry. If you are too angry to have a reasonable discussion with the staff, stop. Often, a calmer approach will get you the results you want. Make an appointment with the administrator or the director of nursing, and try to remember that there is always more than one side to every story.

When preparing to discuss a problem with the nursing home staff, try this approach: First, identify the real problem. It may not be the most recent event, but one that happened three months ago that you didn't say anything about at the time. Come to your meeting with facts, not just feelings. Be prepared to identify events, times, dates, and the personnel involved. Be ready to offer suggestions for improving the situation. At the end of the meeting, tell a key staff member that you would like the administrator to contact you when the situation has been resolved. Don't hesitate to contact the administrator or director of nursing again, if necessary. Remember, you are advocating for your family member and helping him or her get the best possible care.

Get to know the physician and other care providers

All long-term care residents have the right to choose their own healthcare provider; however, residents must select a provider who is a member of the facility's medical staff. The staff can provide a list of physicians/care providers to choose from.

Some physicians and advanced practice nurses specialize in the care of older people. Ask staff if they are familiar with geriatricians or gerontological advanced practice nurses in the area. These healthcare providers may be a good option for you or your loved one to consider.

Long-term care facilities also have medical directors. Often the medical director may work closely with an advanced practice nurse who specializes in the care of older people. Because both the doctor and advanced practice nurse are an integral part of the long-term care team, it's important to develop and maintain a good relationship with them.

If you feel that the healthcare provider you have is not being helpful or does not work well with the nursing home staff, it may be best to choose another one.

The care plan

A care plan is a written description of a resident's care. Think of the care plan as a road map that tells the staff how to reach specific care goals for you or your loved one. Goals that shape care plans may take several forms:

- *Improvement goals* identify a clinical situation that can be improved through care, such as recovery from a broken hip.
- *Maintenance goals* call for a plan to help maintain a resident's current level of functioning.
- *Prevention goals* identify ways to avoid a particular problem, such as complications of diabetes, for which a resident may be at risk.
- *Palliation goals* are used at the end of a person's life, when comfort is the highest priority.

Residents and their families are keys to helping staff design and maintain individualized care plans. In cases where residents are confused, family members often have useful information—the resident's schedule before coming to the facility, medical problems, reactions to medications or treatments, early signs of illness—that the staff may need to be aware of.

Care planning needn't be formal. But it should be ongoing, since the resident's needs will change over time. Casual conversations with staff members can be helpful, as new information is useful to improve care. However, the staff may not always appear to value your input. If you believe that you are offering important information, insist that it be added to the care plan and other permanent records.

In nursing homes, the federal government mandates quarterly care-plan reviews for each resident. By law, residents and their family members may attend these reviews. The care-plan review is your best opportunity to communicate key needs and wishes to the staff. Assisted-living facilities also have care plans and routinely meet to review them. Ask about the care plans and attend the routine meetings with staff.

Although the structure and formality of these meetings may vary, care-plan reviews often involve many members of the long-term care team—a nurse assessment coordinator, activities director, social worker, nurse, dietary manager or dietitian, and various therapists.

Physicians are not usually present because of scheduling complications and reimbursement policies. (Medicare limits payments to physicians for the care of nursing home residents, just as it limits payments for office visits.)

At the meeting, staff members will review the care plan and coordinate efforts to reach each resident's goals. If a resident has a problem with depression and weight loss, for instance, the dietitian may suggest adding nutritional supplements; the social worker may recall the family's willingness to bring in a favorite bedtime snack; the nurse may suggest contacting the pharmacist and physician to change the antidepressant medication; the activities director may plan to be more persistent when inviting the resident to group activities.

Although the care-plan conference is a time for group problem solving, it is generally too brief—families get only ten to fifteen minutes each—for you to air all your concerns. It's best to address most concerns with staff before the meeting. Also, be sure to read the care plan ahead of time—doing so will give you an idea of what kinds of care the staff has planned.

Care plans often are not individualized enough, but you can help address this deficiency by offering suggestions that can only come from you. For example, "Mom would never do crafts, but she is very religious and will likely go to a Bible meeting or other church group. Please see that she goes at least three times each week." If you or your family member have specific ideas for improving care, see that they are noted in the plan.

"You know, I just need someone to help me take care of myself. I want the place really clean, and this is. And I want good food, and we have that. Good food, nice place, and they help take care of me, too."

Follow up on the care plan

State and federal regulations require nursing homes to create and follow care plans. Some assisted-living facilities use them, too. Your job is to review your plan regularly, ask pertinent questions, and request changes that might make it more effective.

Follow up on your requests. It's frustrating, but you may have to request something more than once before it gets done consistently. Don't give up. Ask that your request be added to the care plan or noted somewhere that staff members are likely to see it. For instance, if your loved one prefers card games to bingo, insist that staff members offer activities other than bingo.

Family and resident satisfaction surveys

Most senior housing, assisted-living facilities, and nursing homes ask residents and families to fill out an annual satisfaction survey. It is very important to respond. Your answers may influence future nursing home policy. Satisfaction surveys generally go to both residents and family members. Often, family members who help their loved one complete the survey are surprised by their loved one's answers. Ask the administrator or social worker to share the survey results with you. It will be helpful to see what others think, too. Be sure to continue to follow up on quality of care. Examine quality measures and the quality ratings score at www.medicare.gov (click on "Compare Nursing Homes in Your Area"). Review yearly inspection results for facilities. Periodically use the tools in this book to measure the quality of care in your choice of assisted-living or nursing home facility. It is important to monitor quality of care to be sure you or your loved one are getting the best possible services.

CHAPTER SEVEN

Help Nearby and Nationwide: Ombudsmen, Agencies, and Web Sites

Residents of long-term care facilities have access to an ombudsman, a consumer advocate who investigates and attempts to resolve residents' concerns and complaints. The ombudsman in your area may be able to help you in your search for a good nursing home. He or she will be familiar with many homes in your state and can discuss issues of concern to nursing home residents and their families. In this chapter you will find a state-by-state list of ombudsman programs. You will also find a list of state licensure and certifications programs, as well as a directory of Web sites to help you in your search for good-quality eldercare.

Ombudsman programs

Please note that you can locate your area's ombudsman using the Web site www.ltcombudsman.org/static_pages/help.cfm.

Alabama

State Long-Term Care Ombudsman
Alabama Department of Senior Services
770 Washington Avenue, Suite 470
Montgomery, AL 36130
phone: 334-242-5743
toll-free: 800-243-5463
fax: 334-242-5594

Alaska

State Long-Term Care Ombudsman
Truth Authority Building
3745 Community Park Loop, Suite 200
Anchorage, AK 99508
phone: 907-334-4480
toll-free: 800-730-6393
fax: 907-334-4486

Arizona

State Long-Term Care Ombudsman
Aging and Adult Administration
Department of Economic Security
1789 W. Jefferson Street, 950A
Phoenix, AZ 85007
phone: 602-542-4446
fax: 602-542-6575

Arkansas

State Long-Term Care Ombudsman
Division of Aging and Adult Services
Department of Human Services
P.O. Box 1437, Slot 530
Little Rock, AR 72203
phone: 501-682-2441
fax: 501-682-8155

California

State Long-Term Care Ombudsman
Department of Aging
1300 National Drive, Suite 200
Sacramento, CA 95814
phone: 916-419-7510
fax: 916-928-2503

Colorado

State Long-Term Care Ombudsman
The Legal Center for People with Disabilities and Older People
455 Sherman Street, Suite 130
Denver, CO 80203
phone: 303-722-0300
toll-free: 800-288-1376
fax: 303-722-0720

Connecticut

State Long-Term Care Ombudsman
Department of Social Services
25 Sigourney Street
Hartford, CT 06106
phone: 860-424-5200
toll-free: 866-388-1888
fax: 860-424-4966

Delaware

State Long-Term Care Ombudsman
Division of Services for Aging and Adults with Physical Disabilities
1901 North Du Pont Highway, Main Building
New Castle, DE 19720
phone: 302-577-4791
fax: 302-577-4793

District of Columbia

Long-Term Care Ombudsman for the District of Columbia
Legal Counsel for the Elderly, AARP Foundation
601 E Street Northwest, Building A, 4th Floor
Washington, DC 20049
phone: 202-434-2140
fax: 202-434-6595

Florida

State Long-Term Care Ombudsman
4040 Esplanade Way
Tallahassee, FL 32399
phone: 850-414-2323
toll-free: 888-831-0404
fax: 850-414-2377

Georgia

State Long-Term Care Ombudsman
Division of Aging Services
2 Peachtree Street Northwest
Atlanta, GA 30303
phone: 404-463-8383
toll-free: 888-454-5826
fax: 404-463-8384

Hawaii

State Long-Term Care Ombudsman
Executive Office on Aging
250 South Hotel Street, Suite 406
Honolulu, HI 96813
phone: 808-586-7268

Idaho

State Long-Term Care Ombudsman
Idaho Commission on Aging
3380 American Terrace, Suite 120
PO Box 83720
Boise, ID 83720
phone: 208-334-3833
fax: 208-334-3033

Illinois

State Long-Term Care Ombudsman
Illinois Department on Aging
421 East Capitol Avenue, Suite 100
Springfield, IL 62701
phone: 217-785-3356
toll-free: 800-252-8966
fax: 217-785-4477

Indiana

State Long-Term Care Ombudsman
402 West Washington Street, Room W 454
PO Box 7083, MS21
Indianapolis, IN 46207
phone: 317-232-7134
toll-free: 800-622-4484
fax: 317-232-7867

Iowa
State Long-Term Care Ombudsman
Department of Elder Affairs
510 East 12th Street, Suite 2
Des Moines, IA 50319
phone: 515-725-3333
toll-free: 800-532-3213

Kansas
State Long-Term Care Ombudsman
900 Southwest Jackson, Suite 1041
Topeka, KS 66612
toll-free: 877-662-8362

Kentucky
State Long-Term Care Ombudsman
Department for Aging and
Independent Living
275 East Main Street
Frankfort, KY 40621
phone: 502-564-6930
toll-free: 800-372-2991
fax: 502-564-4595

Louisiana
State Long-Term Care Ombudsman
Governor's Office of Elderly Affairs
PO Box 61
Baton Rouge, LA 70821
phone: 225-342-7100
toll-free: 866-259-4990

Maine
State Long-Term Care Ombudsman
1 Weston Court
PO Box 128
Augusta, ME 04332
phone: 207-621-1079
fax: 207-621-0509

Maryland
State Long-Term Care Ombudsman
Maryland Department of Aging
301 West Preston Street,
Room 1007
Baltimore, MD 21201
phone: 410-767-1100
fax: 410-333-7943

Massachusetts
State Long-Term Care Ombudsman
Executive Office of Elder Affairs
1 Ashburton Place, 5th Floor
Boston, MA 02108
phone: 617-727-7750
toll-free: 800-243-4636
fax: 617-727-9368

Michigan
State Long-Term Care Ombudsman
Michigan Office of Services to
the Aging
PO Box 30676
Lansing, MI 48909
phone: 517-373-8230
fax: 517-373-4092

Minnesota
State Long-Term Care Ombudsman
Minnesota Board on Aging
PO Box 64971
St. Paul, MN 55164
phone: 651-431-2555
toll-free: 800-657-3591

Mississippi
State Long-Term Care Ombudsman
Division of Aging and
Adult Services
750 North State Street
Jackson, MS 39202
phone: 601-359-4929
toll-free: 800-948-3090

Missouri
State Long-Term Care Ombudsman
Department of Health and
Senior Services
PO Box 570
Jefferson City, MO 65102
phone: 573-526-0727
toll-free: 800-309-3282
fax: 573-751-6499

Montana
State Long-Term Care Ombudsman
Office on Aging
Senior and Long-Term Care
Division
Department of Public Health and
Human Services
PO Box 4210
Helena, MT 59604
phone: 406-444-7785
toll-free: 800-332-2272

Nebraska
State Long-Term Care Ombudsman
Health and Human Services
Division of Aging Services
PO Box 95026
Lincoln, NE 68509
phone: 402-471-2307
toll-free: 800-942-7830

Nevada
State Long-Term Care Ombudsman
Department of Health and
Human Services
Division for Aging Services
1860 East Sahara Avenue
Las Vegas, NV 89104
phone: 702-486-3545
fax: 702-486-3572

New Hampshire
State Long-Term Care Ombudsman
Department of Health and
Human Services
129 Pleasant Street
Concord, NH 03301
phone: 603-271-4375
toll-free: 800-442-5640
fax: 603-271-5574

New Jersey
State Long-Term Care Ombudsman
Office of the Ombudsman for the
Institutionalized Elderly
PO Box 852
Trenton, NJ 08625
phone: 609-943-4023
toll-free: 877-582-6995
fax: 609-588-3365

New Mexico
State Long-Term Care Ombudsman
Department of Aging and
Long-Term Care Services
2550 Cerrillos Road
Santa Fe, NM 87505
phone: 505-476-4790
fax: 505-827-7649

New York
State Long-Term Care Ombudsman
New York State Office
for the Aging
1 Empire State Plaza
Albany, NY 12223
phone: 518-474-0108
toll-free: 800-342-9871

North Carolina
State Long-Term Care Ombudsman
Division of Aging and
Adult Services
2101 Mail Service Center
Raleigh, NC 27699
phone: 919-733-3983
fax: 919-733-0443

North Dakota
State Long-Term Care Ombudsman
Aging Services Division
Department of Human Services
600 East Boulevard Avenue,
Department 325
Bismarck, ND 58505
phone: 701-328-4601

Ohio
State Long-Term Care Ombudsman
Ohio Department of Aging
50 West Broad Street, 9th Floor
Columbus, OH 43215
phone: 614-466-1221
toll-free: 800-282-1206

Oklahoma
State Long-Term Care Ombudsman
Aging Services Division
Department of Human Services
2401 NW 23rd Street, Suite 40
Oklahoma City, OK 73107
phone: 405-521-6734
fax: 405-522-6739

Oregon
State Long-Term Care Ombudsman
3855 Wolverine NE, Suite 6
Salem, OR 97305
phone: 503-378-6533
toll-free: 800-522-2602
fax: 503-373-0852

Pennsylvania
State Long-Term Care Ombudsman
Pennsylvania Department of Aging
PO Box 1089
Harrisburg, PA 17108
phone: 717-783-7247

Rhode Island
State Long-Term Care Ombudsman
Alliance for Better Long-Term Care
422 Post Road, Suite 204
Warwick, RI 02888
phone: 401-785-3340

South Carolina
State Long-Term Care Ombudsman
Lt. Governor's Office on Aging
1301 Gervais Street, Suite 200
Columbia, SC 29201
phone: 803-734-9900
toll-free: 800-868-9095
fax: 803-734-9886; 803-734-9887

South Dakota
State Long-Term Care Ombudsman
Department of Social Services
Division of Adult Services
and Aging
700 Governors Drive
Pierre, SD 57501
phone: 605-773-3656
toll-free: 866-854-5465
fax: 605-773-6834

Tennessee
State Long-Term Care Ombudsman
Commission on Aging
and Disability
500 Deaderick Street, Suite 825
Nashville, TN 37243
phone: 615-741-2056
toll-free: 877-236-0013
fax: 615-741-3309

Texas
State Long-Term Care Ombudsman
Texas Department of Aging and
Disability Services
PO Box 149030
Austin, TX 78714
phone: 512-438-3011
toll-free: 800-252-2412

Utah
State Long-Term Care Ombudsman
Aging and Adult Services
120 North 200 West, Room 325
Salt Lake City, UT 84103
phone: 801-538-3910
fax: 801-538-4395

Vermont
State Long-Term Care Ombudsman
Vermont Legal Aid, Inc.
264 N. Winooski Avenue
PO Box 1367
Burlington, VT 05402
phone: 802-863-5620
toll-free: 800-889-2047
fax: 802-863-7152

Virginia
State Long-Term Care Ombudsman
Virginia Association of Area
Agencies on Aging
24 East Cary Street, Suite 100
Richmond, VA 23219
phone: 804-644-2804
fax: 804-644-5640

Washington
State Long-Term Care Ombudsman
Aging and Disability Services
Administration
Department of Social and
Health Services
640 Woodland Square Loop
Lacey, WA 98503
phone: 360-725-2300

West Virginia
State Long-Term Care Ombudsman
West Virginia Bureau of
Senior Services
Commission on Aging
1900 Kanawha Boulevard East
Charleston, WV 25305
phone: 304-558-3317
toll-free: 877-987-3646
fax: 304-558-5609

Wisconsin
State Long-Term Care Ombudsman
Board on Aging and
Long-Term Care
1402 Pankratz Street, Suite 111
Madison, WI 53704
toll-free: 800-815-0015
fax: 608-246-7001

Wyoming
State Long-Term Care Ombudsman
Wyoming Long-Term Care
Ombudsman Program
PO Box 94
Wheatland, WY 82201
phone: 307-322-5553
fax: 307-322-3283

State licensure and certification programs

All nursing homes are licensed by the state in which they are located. Homes that participate in Medicaid or Medicare must also be certified by the state agency responsible for nursing home regulation. The following list of state licensure and certification programs may be useful in your nursing home search, or if you have questions after your loved one moves into a nursing home.

Alabama
Division of Provider Services
Department of Public Health
PO Box 303017
Montgomery, AL 36130
phone: 334-206-5077
fax: 334-206-5088

Alaska
Health Facilities
Certification and Licensing
Department of Health and
Social Services
4730 Business Park Boulevard,
Suite 18
Building H
Anchorage, AK 99503
phone: 907-561-8081
fax: 907-561-3011

Arizona
Division of Assurance and
Licensure Services
Department of Health Services
1647 East Morten Avenue,
Suite 220
Phoenix, AZ 85020
phone: 602-674-4200
fax: 602-861-0645

Arkansas
Office of Long-Term Care
Department of Human Services
PO Box 8059, Mail Slot 402
Little Rock, AR 72203
phone: 501-682-8486
fax: 501-682-6171

California
Licensing and Certification Division
Department of Health Services
PO Box 942732
1800 Third Street, Suite 210
Sacramento, CA 95811
phone: 916-445-3054
fax: 916-445-6979

Colorado
Health Facilities Division
Department of Public Health
and Environment
4300 Cherry Creek Drive South
Denver, CO 80222
phone: 303-692-2819
fax: 303-782-4883

Connecticut
Division of Health
Systems Regulation
Department of Public Health
410 Capitol Avenue,
Mail Slot 12HSR
P.O. Box 340308
Hartford, CT 06134
phone: 860-509-7400
fax: 860-509-7543

Delaware
Division of Long-Term Care
Residents Protection
Department of Health and Social Services
3 Mill Road, Suite 308
Wilmington, DE 19806
phone: 302-577-6661
fax: 302-577-6672

District of Columbia
Health Regulation Administration
825 North Capitol Street Northeast
Washington, DC 20002
phone: 202-442-5888
fax: 202-442-9430

Florida
Division of Health
Quality Assurance
Agency for Health
Quality Administration
2727 Mahan Drive, Room 170,
Mail Stop 9
Tallahassee, FL 32308
phone: 850-487-2528
fax: 850-487-6240

Georgia
Office of Regulatory Service
Department of Human Resources
2 Peachtree Street Northwest,
Suite 21-325
Atlanta, GA 30303
phone: 404-657-5700
fax: 404-657-5708

Hawaii
Office of Health Care Assurance
Department of Health
601 Kamokila Boulevard,
Room 395
Kapolei, HI 96707
phone: 808-692-7420
fax: 808-692-7447

Idaho
Bureau of Facility Standards
Division of Medicaid
Department of Health and Welfare
3380 Americana Terrace, Suite 260
Boise, ID 83720
phone: 208-334-6626
fax: 208-364-1888

Illinois

Office of Health Care Regulation
Department of Public Health
525 West Jefferson Street, 5th Floor
Springfield, IL 62761
phone: 217-782-2913
fax: 217-524-6292

Indiana

Health Care Regulatory
Services Commission
Department of Health
2 North Meridian Street, Section 3B
Indianapolis, IN 46204
phone: 317-233-7022
fax: 317-233-7053

Iowa

Health Facilities Division
Department of Inspections and
Appeals
Lucas State Office Building,
3rd Floor
Des Moines, IA 50319
phone: 515-281-4233
fax: 515-242-5022

Kansas

Bureau of Health Facilities,
Division of Health
Department of Health and
Environment
1000 Southwest Jackson, Suite 330
Topeka, KS 66612
phone: 785-296-1240
fax: 785-296-1266

Kentucky

Division of Long-Term Care
Office of the Inspector General
Cabinet for Health Services
275 East Main Street,
Mail Stop 5E-A
Frankfort, KY 40621
phone: 502-564-2800
fax: 502-562-4268

Louisiana

Health Standards Section
Department of Health and
Hospitals
PO Box 3767
Baton Rouge, LA 70821
phone: 225-342-0415
fax: 225-342-5292

Maine

Division of Licensing and
Certification
Department of Human Services
11 State House Station
442 Civic Center Drive
Augusta, ME 04333
phone: 207-287-9300
fax: 207-287-9304

Maryland

Office of Licensing and
Certification Programs
Department of Health and
Mental Hygiene
55 Wade Avenue
Baltimore, MD 21228
phone: 410-402-8001
fax: 410-402-8215

Massachusetts
Licensure and Certification
Division of Health Care Quality
10 West Street, 5th Floor
Boston, MA 02111
phone: 617-753-8100
fax: 617-753-8125

Michigan
Department of Consumer and Industry Services
Bureau of Health Systems
Division of Health Facility Licensing and Certification
PO Box 30664
525 West Ottawa, 5th Floor
Lansing, MI 48909
phone: 517-241-2626
fax: 517-241-2629

Minnesota
Facility and Provider Compliance Division
Department of Health
PO Box 64900
St. Paul, MN 55164
phone: 651-215-8715
fax: 651-215-8710

Mississippi
Office of Licensure
Health Facilities Licensure and Certification
Department of Health
PO Box 1700
Jackson, MS 39215
phone: 601-576-7300
fax: 601-576-7350

Missouri
Division of Health Standards and Licensure
Department of Health
PO Box 570
912 Wildwood Drive
Jefferson City, MO 65102
phone: 573-751-6271
fax: 573-526-3621

Montana
Quality Assurance, Certification Bureau
Department of Health and Human Services
2401 Colonial Drive, 2nd Floor
PO Box 202953
Helena, MT 59620
phone: 406-444-2099
fax: 406-444-3456

Nebraska
Health Facility Licensure and Inspection
Department of Health
PO Box 95007
Lincoln, NE 68509
phone: 402-471-0179
fax: 402-471-0555

Nevada
Bureau of Licensure and Certification
1550 East College Parkway, Suite 158
Carson City, NV 89710
phone: 702-687-4475
fax: 702-687-6588

New Hampshire
Office of Program Support,
Licensing and Regulation Services
Health Facilities Administration
Department of Health and
Human Services
129 Pleasant Street
Concord, NH 03301
phone: 603-271-4966
fax: 603-271-5590

New Jersey
Long-Term Care Licensing
and Certification
Department of Health and
Senior Services
PO Box 367
Trenton, NJ 08625
phone: 609-633-9034

New Mexico
Health Facility Licensing and
Certification Bureau
2040 South Pacheco, 2nd Floor,
Room 413
Santa Fe, NM 87505
phone: 505-476-9025
fax: 505-476-9026

New York
Office of Continuing Care
Department of Health
166 Delaware Avenue
Delmar, NY 12054
phone: 518-474-1000
fax: 518-478-1014

North Carolina
Certification Section
Division of Facilities Services
Department of Human Resources
PO Box 29530
Raleigh, NC 27626
phone: 919-733-7461
fax: 919-733-8274

North Dakota
Division of Health Facilities
Department of Health and
Consolidated Labs
600 East Boulevard Avenue
Bismarck, ND 58505
phone: 701-328-2352
fax: 701-328-1890

Ohio
Division of Quality Assurance
Department of Health
246 North High Street
Columbus, OH 43266
phone: 614-466-7857
fax: 614-644-0208

Oklahoma
Special Health Services—0237
Department of Health
1000 Northeast 10th Street
Oklahoma City, OK 73117
phone: 405-271-4200
fax: 405-271-3442

Oregon
Client Care Monitoring Unit
Senior and Disabled Services
Department of Human Resources
500 Summer Street, 2nd Floor
Salem, OR 97310
phone: 503-945-6456
fax: 503-373-7902

Pennsylvania
Bureau of Facility Licensure and Certification
Division of Nursing Care Facilities
Room 526, Health and Welfare Building
Harrisburg, PA 17120
phone: 717-787-1816
fax: 717-772-2163

Rhode Island
Division of Facilities Regulation
Department of Health
3 Capitol Hill
Providence, RI 02908
phone: 401-222-2566
fax: 401-222-3999

South Carolina
Bureau of Certification
Department of Health and Environmental Control
2600 Bull Street
Columbia, SC 29201
phone: 803-737-7205
fax: 803-737-7292

South Dakota
Licensure and Certification
Department of Health
615 East 4th Street
Pierre, SD 57501
phone: 605-773-3356
fax: 605-773-6667

Tennessee
Division of Health Care Facilities
Department of Health
425 5th Avenue North
Cordell Hull Building, 1st Floor
Nashville, TN 37247
phone: 615-741-7221
fax: 615-741-7051

Texas
Long-Term Care Regulatory
Department of Human Services
701 West 51st Street
PO Box 149030
Austin, TX 78751
phone: 512-438-2625
fax: 512-438-2726

Utah
Medicare/Medicaid Program
Certification/Resident Assessment
Division of Health Systems Improvement
Department of Health
288 North 1460 West
PO Box 16990
Salt Lake City, UT 84116
phone: 801-538-6559
fax: 801-538-6163

Vermont
Division of Licensing
and Protection
Department of Aging
and Disabilities
103 South Main Street
Waterbury, VT 05671
phone: 802-241-2345
fax: 802-241-2358

Virginia
Center for Quality Health Care
Services and Consumer Protection
Department of Health
3600 West Broad Street, Suite 216
Richmond, VA 23230
phone: 804-367-2102
fax: 804-367-2149

Washington
Residential Care Services
Department of Social and
Health Services
PO Box 45600
Olympia, WA 98504
phone: 360-493-2560
fax: 360-705-6654

West Virginia
Health Facility Licensure
and Certification
Department of Health and
Human Resources
1900 Kanawha Boulevard East,
Building 3, Suite 550
Charleston, WV 25304
phone: 304-558-0050
fax: 304-558-2515

Wisconsin
Bureau of Quality Assurance
Department of Health and Family
Services
PO Box 2969
Madison, WI 53701
phone: 608-267-7185
fax: 608-267-0352

Wyoming
Office of Healthcare Licensing
and Surveys
400 Qwest Building
6101 North Yellowstone Road
Cheyenne, WY 82002
phone: 307-777-7123
fax: 307-777-7127

Helpful Web sites

Of the hundreds of Web sites covering care and services for the elderly, we've handpicked a few of the best. These sites cover nursing home care, financing, annual inspection results, advocacy organizations, and more.

State and federal agencies compile information about each resident living in a Medicare- or Medicaid-certified nursing home. This information is posted on the Web to help you evaluate nursing home quality. Each facility has a "quality measures" report (available for all Medicare- and Medicaid-certified nursing homes). This is a tabulation of the problems experienced by the residents at that particular nursing home. Quality measures quantify such problems as residents needing help with daily activities; having pain, pressure sores, physical restraints, depression or anxiety, loose control of bowel or bladder; having a catheter; spending most of their time in bed or in a chair; having a urinary tract infection; or losing too much weight. Scores for each nursing home are compared with those of other homes in the state. Before visiting a home, you can access the home's quality measures report online at www.medicare.gov and click on the link to compare nursing homes in your area.

Quality ratings range from a low of one star to a high of five stars. You will need to interpret these scores carefully—they may indicate potential problems that require further investigation. The scores are based on survey results, staffing, and quality measures. Similar comparison information is available for certified home health or homecare agencies.

Also, the Administration on Aging Web site has links to state Area Agencies on Aging. These agencies coordinate senior services and eldercare information in each state. If you anticipate a short stay in the nursing home, you may want to contact your local Area Agency on Aging to ask about community services that might help after the senior returns home.

- Administration on Aging:
www.aoa.gov

- American Association of Homes and Services for the Aging, links to state associations:
www.aahsa.org

- American Healthcare Association, links to state associations:
www.ahcancal.org/Pages/Default.aspx

- Links to state Area Agencies on Aging, federal agency consumer Web sites, and other resources:
www.aoa.gov/search/search.asp?q=Area+Agencies+on+Aging

- Another helpful site that lists all home health agencies is Care Pathways:
www.carepathways.com/homecare.cfm

- Centers for Medicare and Medicaid Services contains information about eldercare topics, state-specific Medicaid regulations, and more:
www.cms.hhs.gov/default.asp

- Elders and Families Resources section sponsored by the Administration on Aging:
www.aoa.gov/eldfam/eldfam.asp

- ElderWeb, general long-term care information:
www.elderweb.com/home

- Similar to the nursing home comparison Web site, certified home health or homecare services in all communities are listed by the Centers for Medicare and Medicaid Services. Start by using the Medicare.gov site,
  www.medicare.gov/default.asp

  Then click on "Compare Home Health Agencies in Your Area."

- The National Association of Area Agencies on Aging has helpful links to the regions of each state so that you can locate your local agency for help:
  www.n4a.org/links.cfm

- National Citizens' Coalition for Nursing Home Reform, links to state advocacy groups:
  www.nccnhr.org

- Nursing Home Compare: The Medicare.gov database includes information about every Medicare- and Medicaid-certified nursing home in the United States, and whether the facility has complied with nursing home regulations:
  www.medicare.gov/NHCompare

- To locate the ombudsman in your area:
  www.ltcombudsman.org/static_pages/help.cfm

- Other helpful Web sites when evaluating senior housing include:
  www.aoa.dhhs.gov/eldfam/Housing/Independent_Living/Senior_Apts.asp
  www.calregistry.com/housing/srapts.htm
  www.seniorresource.com/hsoa.htm
  www.aaacap.org/seniornetwork.html

- Other helpful Web sites about assisted living include:
www.helpguide.org/elder/board_care_homes_seniors_residential.htm
www.alfa.org/i4a/pages/index.cfm?pageid=3278
www.aahsa.org/default.asp
www.bjbc.org/page.asp?pgID=209
www.aarp.org/families/housing_choices
www.ltcombudsman.org/static_pages/ombudsmen.cfm

- Other helpful Web sites about nursing homes include:
www.helpguide.org/elder/nursing_homes_skilled_nursing_facilities.htm
www.nursinghomeaction.org
www.advisor.com/boomer/story/plan-effective-senior-facility-care-plan-meeting

ACKNOWLEDGMENTS

No project such as this is undertaken or completed without the support and hard work of many people. First, we want to acknowledge the support of our families and friends who have listened to our ideas and encouraged us to keep going.

Second, we must thank all the residents and their families and friends who contributed their time and experiences to our research, and helped us learn what quality in nursing home care, assisted living, and independent living truly means.

Next, we thank the many independent-living, assisted-living, and nursing home providers and staff who freely shared their invaluable insights with us.

Specifically, we want to thank Dale Smith for his marvelous editorial assistance; he transformed our academic prose into clear, everyday language. And we thank Janine Musick for her articles showcasing our work in *Family Money* magazine and the MIZZOU alumni magazine; her encouragement helped us keep going.

We thank those consumers who have taken the time to read early and later versions of this manuscript; their guidance and insights were critical to this final product. We especially thank Sarah Burger and Meridean Mass, who not only reviewed this book but also wrote the foreword for us.

Others who reviewed and provided wonderful letters of support and encouragement include Dr. Luther Chrisman, retired nursing executive and AARP district coordinator in Nashville, Tennessee; Linda Golodner, president of the National Consumers League; Shawn Bloom, executive director of the National PACE Association; Dr. William H. Thomas, founder of the Eden Alternative; Lucille Vickerman, retired associate administrator of the Rock County Healthcare Center in Janesville, Wisconsin; Dr. Tim Porter-O'Grady, Porter-O'Grady Associates; Dr. Steve Zweig, director, MU Interdisciplinary Center on Aging; Dr. David Oliver, MU Interdisciplinary Center on Aging; and Dr. Cornelia Beck, professor, Department of Geriatrics, University of Arkansas for Medical Sciences, Little Rock.

And, finally, we thank all those who have worked closely with us, offering support, checking on our progress, and working with us on our grants that partially supported the work on these instruments: Drs. Lori Popejoy (who coauthored with us for our first consumer book), Rose Porter, Priscilla LeMone, Roxanne McDaniels, Vicki Conn, Myra Aud, Marcia Flesner, Amy Vogelsmeier, Debra Parker-Oliver, David Mehr, Steve Zweig, Jill Scott-Cawiezell, Jane Bostick, Robin Froman, Greg Petroski, David Zimmerman, Meridean Maas; and also Robyn Smith, De Minner, Carol Siem, Clara Boland, Katy Nguyen, Margie Diekemper and other members of the MU MDS and Quality Research Team.

The members of the MU MDS and Nursing Home Quality Research Team gratefully acknowledge the continuing support of the Missouri Department of Health and Senior Services staff, the Missouri Healthcare Association, and the Missouri Association of Homes and Services for the Aged; they are truly committed to helping homes embrace quality improvement. Research activities were partially supported by NINR 1R01NR/AG05287-01A2. Opinions are those of the authors and do not represent NINR.

ABOUT THE AUTHORS

Marilyn Rantz, RN, PhD, NHA, FAAN
Professor, Sinclair School of Nursing
University Hospitals Professor of Nursing
Director of Aging in Place
Associate Director of the MU Interdisciplinary Center on Aging
Chair of MU MDS and Quality Research Team
University of Missouri
Columbia, Missouri

Dr. Marilyn Rantz is recognized as the country's leading expert on quality of care in nursing homes. She is a licensed nursing home administrator who, for many years, supervised a large county nursing home in southern Wisconsin renowned for its excellent care and services. For years she has conducted quality of care research, consulting widely in the United States and abroad on how to improve the care of older adults.

Currently, Dr. Rantz is the director of Aging in Place, a state-sponsored demonstration project of a new model of long-term care. The project, TigerPlace, is a specially designed independent housing development built to nursing home standards by Americare, with care provided by Sinclair Home Care, a homecare agency initiated by the Sinclair School of Nursing. TigerPlace is the site of numerous cutting-edge research projects focused on developing technologies to help older adults age in the environment of their choice.

She also is associate director of the MU Interdisciplinary Center on Aging and chairs the University of Missouri Minimum Data Set (MDS) and Quality Research Team. She leads multiple research projects focused on understanding and improving the quality of services available to older adults. She is a fellow in the American Academy of Nursing.

Dr. Rantz has written more than one hundred articles or book chapters, as well as several books on quality improvement, health policy, nursing diagnosis, quality assurance, nursing management, and care of the elderly. Three books that she co-wrote have earned Book of the Year awards from the *American Journal of Nursing*: *Quality of Healthcare for Older People in America: A Review of Nursing Studies* (American Nurses Association, 1991), *Outcome-Based Quality Improvement for Long-Term Care: Using MDS, Process, and Outcome Measures* (Aspen Publishing, 1998), and *The New Nursing Homes* (Fairview Press, 2001). The *New Nursing Homes* also won the Sigma Theta Tau International's Research Dissemination to the Public Award in 2003.

Dr. Rantz is committed to helping families find the best nursing homes and other long-term care services. "There are good long-term care settings, including nursing homes, ones with progressive care ideas. The trick is finding the good ones and knowing what to look for. Our walk-through questions for senior housing, assisted living, and nursing homes have been field-tested and found to be extremely helpful to families who face this frequently guilt-ridden decision. Using the walk-through guides to objectively find the best possible care has helped families and residents view long-term care as a blessing in a time of need, rather than a terrifying experience."

Mary Zwygart-Stauffacher, PhD, RN, GNP/GCNS, BC, FAAN
Associate Dean and Professor, College of Nursing and
Health Sciences, University of Wisconsin–Eau Claire,
Gerontological Nurse Practitioner, Red Cedar Clinic/Mayo
Health System, Menomonie, Wisconsin

Dr. Zwygart-Stauffacher is one of the country's leading experts in the care of older adults. She is widely recognized not only for her research skills but also for her clinical expertise with nursing home residents. In addition to her role as associate dean at the University of Wisconsin–Eau Claire, she has a primary care practice with physicians managing residents in nursing homes as an ANCC board-certified gerontological nurse-practitioner and clinical nurse specialist. For more than 25 years, she has worked as an advanced practice gerontological nurse in many teaching, consulting, and practice positions.

She is a former JCAHO surveyor for the long-term care division and is a former member of a technical expert panel for the federal Centers for Medicare and Medicaid Services (CMS) Skilled Nursing Facility Prospective Payment System Quality Medical Review Project. She has consulted with many nursing schools about gerontological nursing curricula and nurse practitioner education. She has also consulted with numerous nursing homes and state quality agencies about quality of care issues and program development.

Dr. Zwygart-Stauffacher is a sought-after researcher and collaborator on nursing home research projects, particularly those examining quality of care. She has written numerous publications and co-written *Outcome-Based Quality Improvement for Long-Term Care: Using MDS, Process, and Outcome Measures* (Aspen Publishing, 1998), which won an *American Journal of Nursing* Book of the Year Award. Dr. Zwygart-Stauffacher explains, "I am concerned about how society can make families feel guilty for not providing all the care that some older adults need. Sometimes, the care is just too much, and the need for it goes on too long for families to do it all themselves. Finding quality long-term care for elders is possible, and moving to a long-term care setting can be the best thing for all involved."